FINDING TRUE NORTH

gone to mc Falls

FINDING TRUE NORTH

Discover your values, enrich your life

MICHAEL HENDERSON

HarperBusiness
An imprint of HarperCollinsPublishers

To Shar
(Primary!)
I love you

National Library of New Zealand Cataloguing-in-Publication Data

Henderson, Michael, 1963-
Finding true north : discover your values, enrich your life /
Michael Henderson.
Includes bibliographical references.
ISBN 1-86950-472-0
1. Values clarification. 2. Conduct of life. 3. Work ethic. I. Title.
170—dc 21

Harper*Business*
An imprint of HarperCollins*Publishers*

First published 2003
HarperCollins*Publishers (New Zealand) Limited*
P.O. Box 1. Auckland

ISBN 1 86950 472 0

Designed and typeset by Graeme Leather
Printed by Griffin Press, Australia on 70 gsm Bulky Book Ivory

The most important thing is to know what is the most important thing.

Happiness is directly related to how we focus our mental energy and values.

Paul Chippendale, Values Education Network

Acknowledgements

A very special thank you to my wife Shar for helping to make my North, True. I love you.

To Mum and Dad for being who you are.

To Irene Wilson for sowing the seeds all those years ago.

Special thanks to: Steve Phillips for his enduring friendship, words of wisdom and financial support and belief in our work over the past six years; Bill MacLeod for his friendship, advice and support over many years, especially when the going was tough ('interesting'); and Peter Dalton for his support, friendship, inspiration, belief in the E-myth process and most importantly a huge heart.

A galactic-size thanks to Paul Chippendale for his saintly patience, knowledge, generosity, sharing, commitment, innovation, pioneering spirit and friendship.

To the thousand of participants on True North workshops, you have added so much to the journey.

I would also like to thank: Sherryll Gates for her support, interest, friendship and involvement; the Teiho family, especially Auntie Bubs and Mr T — we wouldn't be here without you; Bharat Mistry at ASB Business Banking for timely advice and willingness to listen to a small New Zealand company with a big dream; Jenny Nicholson for her amazing discipline and efforts to get us where we needed to be; Dr Cathie Dunsford for her advice, passion and belief in this book; Sheila Alexander for her patience and accuracy in proofreading the manuscript; Sarah Williams for feedback on writing style and content; David and Annie Walden for the use of their hideaway 'Hilton', the perfect environment to convert notes into text; the Spice Café on Waiheke Island for their ongoing friendliness and hospitality and delicious date scones; and finally, the team at HarperCollins for making this all so easy. A special thank you to Tracey Wogan and Sue Page for making the readable understandable.

Contents

Part Three
Never let the things that matter most to you be at the mercy of those that do not

HOW TO USE THIS BOOK

Welcome to *Finding True North*. This book is designed to help you discover your personal values and apply them to your life.

I would encourage you to read the whole book first before beginning the exercises, although it is a good idea to make a note of any thoughts or inspirations you have along the way.

Living your values is not a quick fix for the problems in your life. It takes time and will probably require you to make changes in the way you live. Some changes may not be easy, but you'll get there with patience and perseverance.

If you have questions about the book, you can contact me by email at truenorth@valuesatwork.org

May your North be True,
Michael Henderson

INTRODUCTION

Lessons from the desert

We have stories to tell, stories that provide wisdom about the journey of life. What more have we to give one another than our 'truth' about human adventure as honestly and as openly as we know how!

Rabbi Saul Rubin

I found myself lost in the desert. I was part of an overland trip, travelling through Africa in a converted army truck, from Morocco in the north to Cape Town in the south.

We'd made good progress through the northern Sahara and were camped one evening somewhere between the watering-hole villages of In Salah and Arak in Algeria. Having spent over eight hours sitting in the truck that day, I decided to go for a run across the barren terrain to iron out the kinks and numbness in my body.

I was wearing a pair of running shoes, a sleeveless T-shirt and shorts, and had a compass hanging around my neck. I ran for about fifteen minutes, by which time the sun was starting to set. I turned back in the direction of the camp and, after checking my compass direction, set off running again. Within fifteen minutes the sun had disappeared and night descended upon the desert with the suddenness of a light being switched off. I checked the fluorescent points of the compass and ran on again for another five minutes, calling out in the darkness to my friends and peering about for any sign of light from the camp.

My yelling was pointless. In the Sahara, once the sun has set, it is common for the desert wind to roar across the barren terrain, blocking out sounds and taking the temperature from 60° Celsius just before sunset to subzero temperatures not long after. I continued to run for a further five minutes before it occurred to me that I might have a serious problem, as I knew next to nothing about how to survive in the desert at night.

This seemed ironic because I had recently completed my degree at university, which I had presumed would provide me with all the information and knowledge I would require to make my way in the world. However, circumstances were quick to prove that a Bachelor of Arts degree from Auckland University was worth diddly-squat (i.e. not a lot) in my current predicament. It occurred to me that an education and practical know-how really are two very different things.

I decided that I should keep running to ward off hypothermia. Despite being very fit at the time, I only lasted for what must have been a couple of hours. As I neared exhaustion, I began to feel courage and hope evaporate. I collapsed to my knees and decided to dig a hole, jump in and cover myself with sand to keep warm. (Like all truly misguided insights, it seemed like a good idea at the time!)

It seemed to take forever to dig the hole as the ground was rock hard, and I kept cutting my fingers and tearing off bits of fingernails, which stung badly in the icy wind. Eventually I had dug a hole big enough to lie in and it was at this point that I realised what I had done . . .

The only thing missing was a tombstone.

I began to panic. I had no idea how I was going to keep warm long enough either to find my way back to the camp or for people from the camp to find me. It began to dawn on me that I might actually die. The moment I registered this as a possibility, I felt a sense of terror that began as a cold metallic sensation in the pit of my stomach. Gradually it crawled through my bones and across my flesh to chill the surface of my skin. I had never been so afraid in my life (that was, of course, before I returned home again and experienced driving on New Zealand's roads).

I was still on my knees, when somewhere in my warped sense of reality I heard a little voice. It sounded like a terribly shy child at the back of the classroom who suddenly realises they know the answer to the teacher's question and slowly plucks up the courage to raise a hand and voice an insight. It spoke slowly and softly to me, with a degree of uncertainty, as if it was exploring the idea for itself: 'What if the fact that you are this terrified of dying actually means something else?'

I was feeling so disoriented and distracted by external events that I found it difficult to even understand the question. Fortunately the little voice did not wait for my answer and continued. 'Perhaps,' it said, 'the main reason you are experiencing this intense resistance to dying is actually an indication of the immense desire you still have to live.'

My initial reaction to the thought was sarcastic. 'No kidding, Sherlock.' Apparently the little voice did not understand overt sarcasm, because it carried on. 'All this emotion you are currently experiencing as fear could be renamed "an intense passion for life".'

This flash of the obvious covered me reassuringly like a warm blanket. Of course! If I did not want to die, it was logical to assume I must want to live. Even writing this now, it sounds crazy. Yet at the time, that one thought shifted my emotional state from one of panic and terror into pure exhilaration and passion. My internal resources rallied around this thought like volunteers around an inspired leader and offered to do whatever it took to make it out of the desert. At a time of impending death, I suddenly felt so very alive!

Taking advantage of the sudden rush of adrenaline, I began to think like a survivor and dedicated all my mental energy to thinking about the pleasant things in my life that I enjoyed and celebrated. I contemplated the things that made my life worth living, that I was passionate about, that were important to me. In fact, what I began to do, without realising it, was to compile my very first personal values inventory. I later learned that values can be defined as our lifestyle preferences and priorities. These have since become the cornerstone of my life and my work.

I considered the things I still wished to achieve in life. I thought about the things that made my life fulfilling and exciting, that inspired me, that gave my life meaning. It was by considering what it was I valued that I found an ever-increasing determination to save my own life.

Determination to live coursed through my body. Now was not my time to die; now was my time to live, to reach out and grasp life with both hands, to reclaim it fully, determinedly, passionately. I took a last look at the grave I had dug for myself, staggered to my feet and jogged slowly through the night, moving at a sufficient pace to keep my body temperature high enough to stop me from freezing.

My sudden lift in spirit, energy and determination seemed

almost miraculous. I did not know at that time that the Latin root word for values is *valor*, meaning strength. It is our values that give us meaning in life, and meaning in turn provides us with strength, motivation and willpower. In understanding our values, we equip ourselves with a perennial source of motivation, focus and strength to achieve those things that matter most to us. It was that strength that kept me running.

As I ran, I planned my future in values-laden detail, imagining all the meaningful things I wanted to achieve in my life. My running fell into a rhythm and I envisaged myself as an author telling this story. I imagined becoming a teacher of some type and travelling the world to share my ideas with like-minded people. I imagined living a life of meaning, filled with passion, work and laughter.

What I began to realise was that there were only a few things I valued that really made a difference in my life. They were the fundamentals — the things that really made life worth living. I considered the possibility that they were also the things by which I measured my own life. The things I valued were fun and humour, learning, travel, creativity, adventure and people. Although I did not recognise these things as values at the time, I did understand their motivational power. I recognised, too, that by simply focusing on any of these things I could, within moments, transcend my immediate situation and transform my emotional and mental state — even my sense of identity. This shift in viewpoint — from seeing myself as a tragic victim of circumstance to a survivor of an adventure with a story to share — I credit to this day as being the reason I made it out of the desert alive. My mind went on building my perfect future while my body staggered through the wind, cold and darkness. It was due to my occupied state of mind and the darkness that I neglected to notice the cliff edge!

I went sailing off into midair with my legs still running beneath me like some character in an animated cartoon. From a childhood nightmare, an old familiar and terrible feeling followed of endlessly falling into darkness. I hit the ground hard, exploding the wind from my lungs, and slid face-first down a gravel slope, which despite the numbness from the cold felt like a naked slide over a cheese grater (not that I have verified that by putting the metaphor to the test).

I still do not really understand what happened next, but I am eternally grateful that it did. Despite being severely winded, I began to laugh. The thought of my running into midair off the cliff and plummeting to the gravel below somehow seemed very funny. The laughing forced air back into my lungs, and lifted my spirits. Nietzsche's words, 'That which does not kill me makes me stronger', began to whirl in my mind like a mantra while I slowly regained some composure and climbed back to my feet. I was grazed quite badly from the fall, and my cold muscles were beginning to cramp severely. I hugged myself tightly to fight the cold.

As I stood there trying to gain a sense of direction, I slowly became aware of an eerie feeling of being watched. Goosebumps rose quickly as I darted my eyes in all directions, trying to locate the source of this intrusive gaze. I could see no one, and eventually in frustration I yelled out, 'Who are you? Show yourself!'

I paused and waited for a response. It came a few seconds later. 'Who are you? Show yourself! . . . Who are you? Show yourself! . . . Who are you? Show yourself!' It took several repetitions before I realised it was an echo. In a bizarre, almost metaphysical manner, my own question had come back to challenge me: 'Who are you? Show yourself!' Somehow the question disoriented me, and for a moment I actually had no idea who I really was. Sure, I knew my name, my history, my habits, my likes and dislikes. However, I became aware that I did not *really* know who I was. 'How bizarre,' I thought to myself as I began to jog again to fight off the cold. 'I wonder who I am? I mean, *really*, who am I?' I wondered if there might be a connection between what I considered most important to me and how I defined myself. I suspected there was.

After what felt like several hours of running, I saw a light on the horizon. I ran on towards it for some time and finally realised they were the lights from what I suspected was an airfield. This was confirmed an hour later when I ran into the electric security fence, which I had failed to notice because of the blinding effect of the runway lights.

After I had recovered from the electrical shock I was able to climb the fence, as it must have blown a fuse somewhere and the fence had shorted out. What I didn't realise was that the fence was only loosely attached to the two vertical standing support poles about six metres apart on either side of me. I have always appreciated the fact that humour has a way of emerging in my life every time the logical or expected is interrupted by the inexplicable and unexpected. I began to giggle to myself, as the higher I climbed up the fence, the closer I got to the ground. My body weight pulled the already loose mesh fence away from the support poles and by the time I was halfway up the fence, I was only a metre or so off the ground, hanging parallel to the sand and looking directly into the night sky.

I was laughing so much by this time that I could hardly hold on, and by the time I made it to the top of the fence, I was lying flat on my back in the gravel with the fence lying over me like a giant crocheted steel blanket.

I paused at this point to enjoy the ridiculous nature of my situation and then managed to climb out from underneath the fence and stagger across the airfield to be found, eventually, by an Algerian soldier. I suppose he was on guard duty, although I was practically on top of him by the time he noticed me. I suspect he had been asleep. My sudden appearance startled him and in a defiant effort to regain his composure, he grabbed me by the arm and began yelling at me in what I presumed was a Berber dialect. He then dragged me off to a nearby hut to meet his sergeant.

I spent the rest of the night being interrogated (the sergeant later referred to this as 'interviewed') by a never-ending supply of soldiers, military police and what looked like members of the French Foreign Legion. Of course, in the interest of French and Algerian national security, I can neither confirm nor deny that what I think I saw was actually what I did see.

Around dawn they must have decided that a shredded, bleeding, frozen fool was no threat to national security or macho reputations, so they graciously let me sleep curled up under a newspaper on the sergeant's table. I was awoken a couple of hours later by a sharp prod in the ribs. More interrogation followed, this time surrounded by a large number of personnel who left me with the impression I was less the focus of an interrogation process and more the star of a curiosity show. Everyone was laughing and joking except me. I just wanted more sleep.

After several hours they took me outside and pointed to a truck driving across the desert towards us. It was the group I was travelling with. On arrival they were delighted and relieved to see me (except, perhaps, the ones who had enjoyed the extra food rations in my absence). They bundled me into the truck, wrapped me up in blankets, poured cold soup down me and let me sleep for the remainder of the day. Later that evening I was awarded the inaugural 'Wally Award'.

I am not particularly proud to admit that at the end of the trip

I won the award outright (voted by my peers) for having committed the stupidest act on the entire journey. I prefer to think of it as unfortunate rather than stupid, yet in fact it was actually very fortunate as it proved to be a significant incident in my life. On reflection, that incident was the first of several that brought to my awareness the unsettling but inescapable fact that we are all only temporary visitors to this world, and the experiences we have are influenced as much by our attitude and choices as by our circumstances and environment.

Some of the wonder of travel is that during time spent far away from all that is familiar to us we can discover aspects of ourselves that we might otherwise never locate due to their being submerged in our habitual living patterns. By observing and listening to ourselves in these unfamiliar surroundings we are able to see and hear parts of our characters we might otherwise ignore.

Whenever I recall the whole desert episode now, I can view it quite objectively. I can see I had an additional perspective, watching myself go through it. I have come to some powerful realisations about the adventure of creating myself that I would not have dreamed possible during, or even for some time after, those events. I refer to these realisations or insights rather dramatically as 'the lessons from the desert'. Three of these lessons form the basis of this book and my philosophy of life.

Lesson One

The most important thing is to know what is the most important thing

The reason so many of us change after life-influencing events is that we are forced to reassess our priorities in life. We must stop our habitual busyness and examine our deeper values. During these events we are also forced to rely on something other than our logical and habitual thinking. We awaken ourselves to the possibility of our own intuition — our own inner teaching.

When we begin to establish what is important, we begin to create meaning in our lives. This meaning, once established and embraced, has the effect of shedding light on who we are. The challenging situations we create for ourselves are not bad or unfortunate; each can be an opportunity to awaken us and provide insight into our lives so we can experience ourselves fully. These situations provide opportunities to reflect on our character, purpose, identity, values, capabilities and behaviours. All these things, when contemplated together, help us identify who we are. We can then decide what we like and wish to maintain, and what we will change or replace with something more in line with who we are or want to be.

Lesson Two

Who are you? Show yourself!

Being alone in the desert at night affords you an amazing view of the night sky. Uninhibited by the lights from a city or even a campfire that usually dim our view of the stars' light, the visual effect is magical in its scope and grandeur.

As I stared at the countless stars, I gradually became aware that I was just one and they numbered in the millions. I am sure many of us have had this experience in our lives. What was different for me this time was that I was lost and alone.

The overwhelming effect of staring up into the sparkling celestial city, making me feel so small, so insignificant, swamped by the universe — coupled with the feeling of being more alone than I had ever been in my life — gave birth to an insight.

Our sense of loneliness is not a result of the lack of others, it is a result of lacking a sense of self. The more we lack a sense of self, the more we feel alone. It was the realisation that I lacked a sense of self that sparked my determination to begin the journey of really understanding who I am.

By determining our personal values, we can gain a clearer understanding of who we are. This in turn slowly leads to an underlying impression that, unlike our relationship to the stars where we feel like only one *of* a million, we begin to enjoy our uniqueness, the experience of being one *in* a million — not in an egotistical, arrogant way, but in a way that makes us feel that we are unique and yet still part of the whole grand design that is life. Our values make our meaning and our sense of self measurable.

Lesson Three

Never let the things that matter most to you be at the mercy of the things that do not

In the desert I learned the importance of having a reason to live, other than just to avoid dying. Finding a passion for life was empowering enough to displace things such as fear, pain, fatigue and cold. Yet people often place things that are of secondary importance to them ahead of what they truly value.

A common example of this is people who work so hard they very rarely see their families or get quality time with them, and yet their families are their highest value. Such values conflicts are the source of much frustration and stress and, until resolved, inflict a heavy burden.

The key to avoiding such values conflicts is to be really clear about your priorities and align these with all aspects of your life.

This book will show you how to establish your values, and in doing so you will also learn to:

- create and experience a deeper sense of meaning in your life
- invest your time more effectively
- live your life on your own terms
- make better decisions for yourself
- experience a stronger sense of self
- boost your self-esteem
- reduce your stress levels
- plan more effectively and set appropriate goals for yourself
- be more tolerant of others
- experience more happiness and feel more fulfilled
- experience personal growth
- locate layers of simplicity in your life below the surface of the complexities of modern life
- love yourself.

Self-love is not so vile a seed as self-neglect.

William Shakespeare

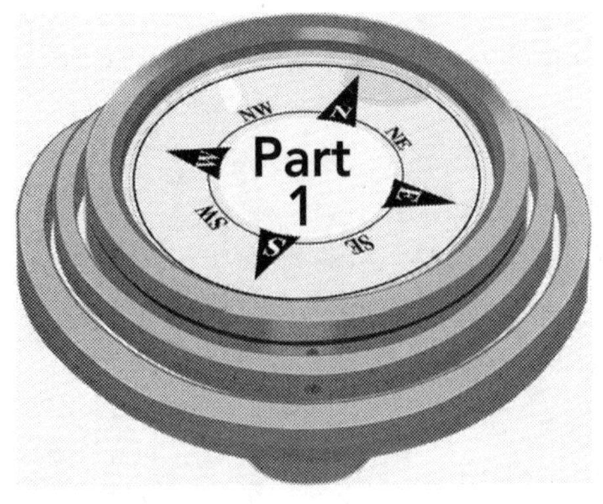

The most important thing is to know what is the most important thing

CHAPTER 1

What are values?

Values are your preferences and priorities.

Everyone has values. Our values are our personal preferences and priorities. Values represent what is most important to us in life. Some examples are: health, security, relaxation, acceptance, family and respect.

Values are abstract concepts, and as such we can only know that values are really in our lives when we experience living in accordance with them. Values are intangible, which means we cannot touch our values as physical objects because they do not exist in the physical world; our values are ideas that enable us to prioritise our experiences with the world around us. For example, the value 'security', although not a physical object, is a concept that we can all relate to and on which many of us place great importance. The amount of importance we place on security in our lives can be identified by what we spend our money on, how we behave, the choices we make about where to live, the job we do, where and when to travel, what type of car to own and which people to associate with. Although values are not physical objects, physical objects can represent values to us.

Through the ownership or presence of a physical object, we can experience our values. Owning a house, for example, may represent a number of values for us. The following list suggests some values that a house might represent to an individual: security, achievement, art/beauty, economics/profit, family belonging.

This distinction between values and physical objects is an important one to understand, because it influences how we determine our personal values. To help clarify this point still further, try this simple exercise. Look at the physical objects listed in the column on the left in the table opposite, none of which are actually values. Alongside these objects, write down some of the words that these objects represent to you. You might choose to browse through the appendix at the end of this book to help you identify some of the values you associate with these objects.

The words you have written in the right-hand column are the values you associate with the physical objects. If the physical objects with which we surround ourselves and fill our lives are to have any real meaning, they must represent our deeper values. It is useful to clarify the values behind an object because often there are ways in which you can achieve the same values through other activities, thoughts, behaviours and objects. For example, you may gain a greater sense of the value of security, not by owning a larger house, but by spending more quality time with the people who live in your current house. It is the meaning behind the objects that shows the real importance of the items to us.

What creates and influences our values?

Our beliefs influence and create our values. For example, having family as a life priority is determined by the underlying belief that we would rather have family than be deprived of that experience.

Representation of values by physical objects

OBJECT	UNDERLYING MEANING OR VALUE
HOUSE	SECURITY
CAR	TRANSPORT
CDS	
MONEY	FOOD
CLOTHES	WARM

The diagram below indicates the various influences on our values and how our values in turn have an influence on other aspects of our lives.

The diagram shows how the core influences on our values are our world-view, or underlying assumptions about life, and our belief systems. From here we have a wide range of cultural, psychological, technical and environmental contributions to the formation of our values. If we look at the outer ring of the figure, we can see how this works. Let's take media as an example of external factors. If through various forms of media we begin to believe that the world is an unsafe place and there are dangers all around us, then we will prefer to live our lives in certain ways —

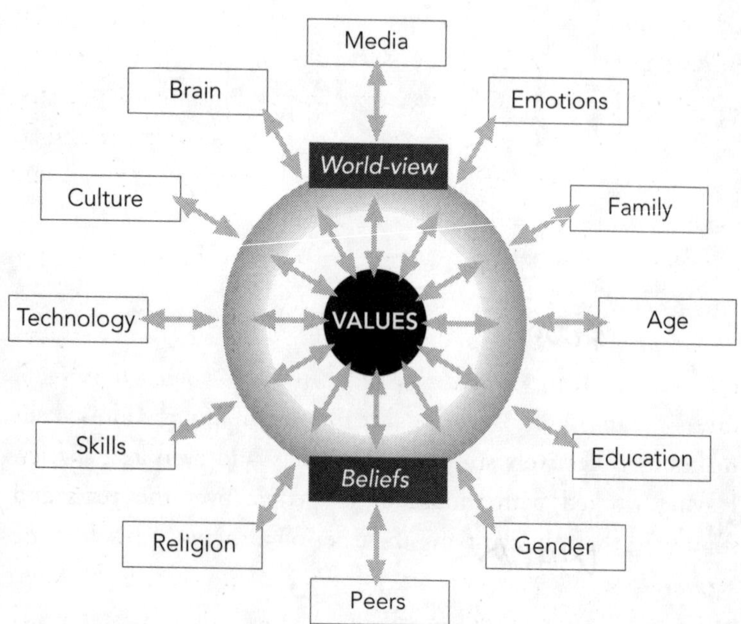

Influences on our values; values influencing our lives

Adapted with permission from Paul Chippendale, © The Minessence Foundation

it will affect how we travel, where we live, who we associate with. These values are based on a set of beliefs influenced by the media. Likewise, if through various forms of media we begin to believe that the world is a safe, fun adventure playground, then similarly we will prefer to live our lives in ways that reflect that set of beliefs.

When I first studied with Paul Chippendale, founder of the International Values Education Network, to become a master trainer of values, he emphasised the point that although it is interesting to be aware of where values come from, he placed a greater importance on an individual's ability to ensure that they had a genuine and authentic relationship with each value. What he meant by this was that as individuals we are likely to pick up on the values of others through the media, fashion, religion, education, peer pressure and so on. This is a natural part of belonging to a culture; however, we should clarify for ourselves whether the value is really important to us or whether we are just buying into other people's values in order to be accepted and fit in. Living values that are not our own is disempowering and forces us into making choices and decisions based on criteria other than our own. This leads to frustration, resentment, disempowerment and lowered self-esteem.

Chippendale suggests that the benefit to each of us in developing our own chosen values is that it creates 'strength through diversity'. In other words, the fact that we are unique individuals makes us collectively stronger as a society and even as a species. Having worked with thousands of people over the years and supported them in clarifying their personal values, it has become very clear to me that understanding personal values is far more useful to people and society at large than a study of the financial worth that material objects are said to possess. It is our values in fact that determine the financial worth of all material objects, and even the value of our life experiences. This is because our values link together our thoughts, feelings and actions to create meaning.

Why values are so important

Whenever people achieve personal success with their goals, relationships, work, sport, art, education, finance, parenting and so on, they do so because they are applying the Head, Heart, Hands model, although of course they may not realise this is what they are doing. The model shows that in order for us to experience personal success in any of our endeavours there are three key areas that contribute to our success. These are:

- our Focus, which means where our head is at (Head).
- our Motivation, or what we have the heart for (Heart).
- our Capability, which refers to our skills and abilities and what we can handle (Hands).

Personal success with Head, Heart and Hands

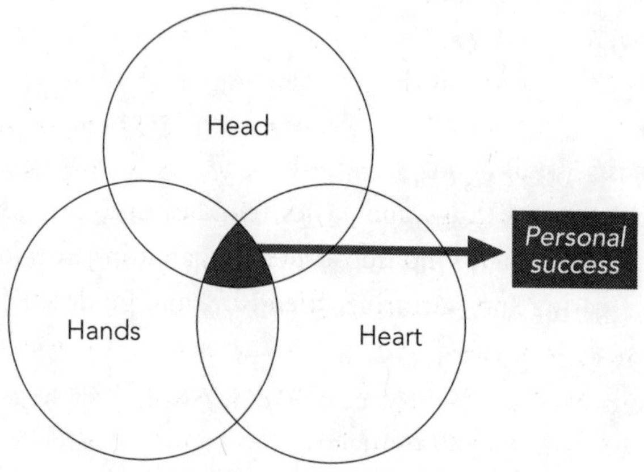

Diagram adapted with permission from Paul Chippendale

When we have all three of these areas working together we experience personal success.

For example, if you want to experience success as a netball or rugby player, the Head, Hands and Heart model could be useful. In order to succeed you will need to understand the rules of the game, the tactics and strategies involved, the coach's instructions and you will also need to focus and concentrate. These things are all to do with the Head — knowledge, understanding, focus and attention. Likewise you will need skills and techniques, and hand and body dexterity. These are the Hands aspects of your recipe for success. Finally you will need some attitude — motivation, desire and drive. This is the Heart aspect. It is only when all three things operate together that we experience personal success and have a peak experience on the inside whilst delivering peak performance on the outside.

Sportspeople often describe this situation as being 'in the zone'. Although we have used a sports example in this description the model applies equally well to any facet of human interest that you wish to do well at. It applies to friendship, parenting, study, work, finance, gardening, any hobby, spirituality, any sport, in fact anything you care to mention, including learning to live in alignment with your values.

For example, parenting requires knowledge, understanding and focus (Head). It also requires hands-on involvement with dressing, cleaning, hugs and kisses, cuddles and play (Hands). And of course there's no substitute in parenting for love and affection, caring and nurturing, friendship and guidance (Heart).

Likewise, to succeed with our finances we again need knowledge and information, such as how and where to invest (Head). We need skills, such as completing tax returns and working out investment rates (Hands). We also need to manage our emotions around money, and have a desire to successfully manage our finances (Heart).

By examining the following three diagrams we can quickly see what happens if one of these three elements is missing.

If you have the Hands and the Heart without the Head, then you *may* act, but you are likely to just run around in all directions, doing unrelated things and accomplishing little of significance.

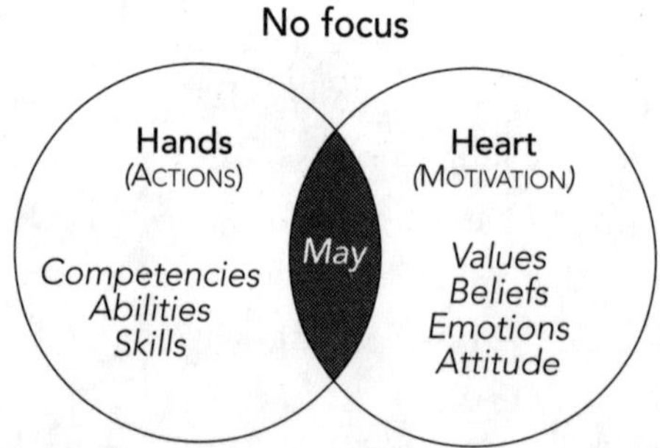

If you have the Hands and the Head without the Heart, you *could* act — but probably won't, because although you have the focus and the capabilities, you lack the motivation.

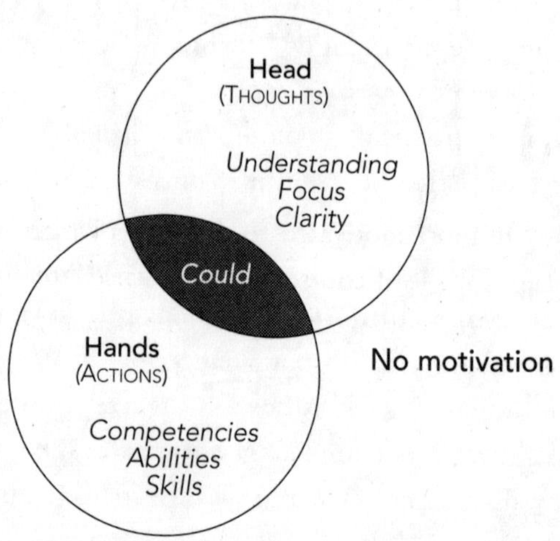

If you have the Head and the Heart without the Hands, you *would* act, but you're unable to, because you do not have the necessary skills, abilities or resources.

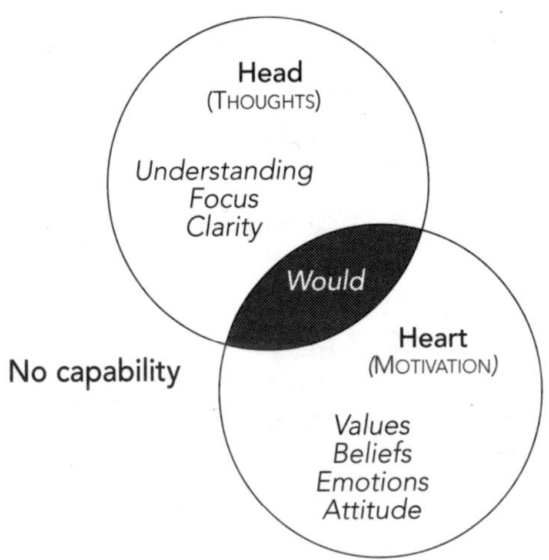

It is only when you have Head, Heart and Hands all acting together that you *will* act effectively. This is where values come in:

Head: You attain focus through personal values clarity. When what you wish to focus on is related to what is most important to you (i.e. your values) it's easier to stay focused.

Heart: You are most motivated to do things which match your values. This is of course common sense. You are far more likely to be motivated by things that are important to you than by things that are not.

Hands: You prefer to gain skills and abilities around things relating to your values.

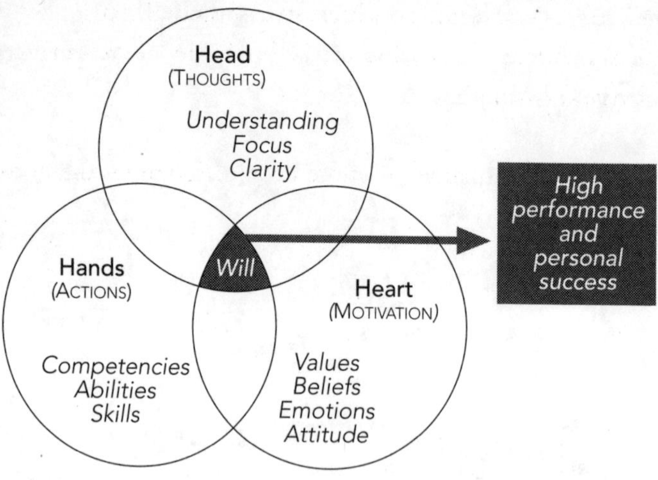

Here are some final points on why values are important to us in some very practical ways:

- Our values, when understood, provide us with a clearer and deeper sense of who we are.
- Values create meaning in our lives and form the basis for our motivation; something that is not valued will not motivate us.
- Values are the mechanism through which we make evaluations and decisions; they tell us what is important and when to say yes or no.
- Values focus our attention. Notice that when something is not important to you, it is more difficult to concentrate on it and often your attention wanders. Our values direct our energy. When we value something we put our physical, emotional, financial and mental energy into it.

- Our successful relationships are always built on compatible or shared values. What we love represents our deepest values.

These points are explained in more detail throughout the book.

CHAPTER 2

What values are not

If you stand, stand.
If you sit, sit.
Above all, don't wobble.

Ummon Zen Master

The reason so many people seem to have difficulty effectively experiencing their values in life and making them work is that they often get values mixed up with other philosophical or linguistic terms such as morals and ethics, principles and virtues. It appears that half the effort of accurately defining what values are is to clarify what they are *not*.

This chapter covers the most common areas often confused with values. This is an important chapter to read if you are interested in determining your own personal values, as it will help you avoid some of the most common mistakes inadvertently made by people when working with values. You will be assisted in determining your personal values by using the guidelines outlined in later chapters.

Ethics

Ethics are agreed codes of behaviour adopted by an association of people who are interested primarily in ensuring there are guidelines for behaviour and actions for the group's members. Hence, doctors and lawyers have ethical codes of practice, which they swear to uphold as part of their professional behaviour. An ethical decision is one that typically involves choosing between what you have agreed not to do and what you now find yourself wanting to do.

Morals

Morals are our adopted viewpoints pertaining to judging what is good and bad. Morals define for us what is right and what is wrong. Someone who is described as being morally corrupt or lacking in morals is judged as acting, thinking or behaving in a manner that the observer defines as bad, wrong or inappropriate in some way. A moral decision typically involves choosing between two options: one you perceive to be right and the other wrong.

Principles

Principles are time-tested truths of a natural, scientific or man-made nature, for example, the scientific principle of gravity. Individuals may have their own personal principles, time-tested, self-imposed or adopted truths they have incorporated as rules to obey in their own lives.

Judgements

Judgements are labels representing our beliefs, which usually have more to say about us than they do about what is labelled. To judge someone's values is to have a moral perspective on their values. For example, saying someone is 'ugly' is a judgement based on your personal beliefs about beauty, and it also implies you consider being ugly to be wrong.

Virtues

Virtues are personality traits or characteristics, such as courage, patience or politeness, that people or cultures hold in high regard. They are deemed to be favourable or the 'right' way to be. A value by contrast is a personal preference, that may or may not meet with society's wider approval. Virtues can be observed as behaviours or actions. Values on the other hand are strictly concepts that we use in order to evaluate the relevance, appropriateness or effectiveness of our behaviours. They are not the behaviours themselves.

When someone acts courageously, they can be said to have the virtue of courage. Values, on the other hand, cannot be owned or attributed to a person as part of their personality make-up. We can only say that a person acted in accordance with a particular value. You might think of a virtue as being like a personal possession, that is admired by others, whereas a value is your own unique and particular guiding star. The line of distinction between these two is often a thin one, and if you wish to clarify any specific virtues to determine their values content, I suggest you refer to the appendix at the end of this book which lists 125 global values.

Attitudes

An attitude refers to a reactive response to environmental stimulants. An attitude is an expression of our beliefs and personality through thoughts, behaviour, words, gestures or sounds. Attitudes can be an expression of our values.

Needs

Needs are resources, actions or behaviours that are required to experience our values. For example, if health is a value we choose to experience in our lives, then we will need to eat sensibly, exercise regularly, sleep well and think positively. The needs are the ingredients — the value is the experience.

What we value and what we need are often two very different things. For example, when cigarette smokers say they need to stop smoking because of their health, that doesn't necessarily mean they *will* stop smoking unless they value their health more than they value continuing to smoke.

If you live in a country where your needs can be relatively easily addressed, then your life takes on a 'what would I like and want' perspective — a values perspective — far more than one of 'what do I need'. In other words, once our basic needs are met, life becomes more about our personal preferences and priorities (our values) than it does about needs. Our values indicate those things that are wanted, desired and preferred.

I have arrived at the opinion that in fact we *need* nothing. We do not even need oxygen — unless, of course, you prefer to stay alive. This may sound obvious, yet it is not. I live in a nation with the second-highest youth suicide rate per capita in the world. If we wish to stay alive, that is a preference, not a need. When you look at your supposed needs, you may well find they are not needs at all — they are simply your preferences.

Recent research on needs shows they relate closely to values. In his book *Control Theory,* William Glasser suggests humans have only four predominant requirements in life: love, fun, mastery and freedom. How we go about achieving these four basic needs varies from person to person, determined by individual preferences and priorities. How I gain a sense of loving and being loved may differ significantly from how you do this.

Beliefs

Beliefs are a critical area to be aware of when working with values. In many respects, a value is simply an established belief about the desirability, preference and priority of something. The belief, in fact, creates the value, as our values are nothing more than a representation of our underlying belief systems. For anything we value, we must have a belief that it is important to us for some reason. For example, if we value recreation, it is only because we believe recreation is of benefit to us. Likewise, anything we deem to have low or no value is predetermined by a belief.

Harry Palmer, the author and developer of a wonderful book about beliefs, *Resurfacing*, suggests that if you study anything in enough detail you are studying a belief. The definition of beliefs that I like to work with is that they are our expression of the degree of certainty we have about something. Things that we have a high degree of certainty about will be reflected by a strongly held belief. However, matters about which we know nothing or have some doubt about where we stand will be reflected by a weaker sense of belief. Our degree of certainty simply indicates how much energy we will put into the belief.

Emotions

Values are not emotions. Emotions are feelings, while values are concepts. Our values are our specific ideas about what we hold to be important or meaningful to us. Emotions are how we feel about those values. Therefore happiness, for example, is not a value. Happiness is an emotion, one of many that we could experience in relation to any of our values — we might feel happy to experience security, just as we might also feel fear, frustration or regret when we do not.

Throughout this book, emotions are considered particularly important because they are a key indicator as to which values are most important to us. The more strongly you feel about the value, the more important it is likely to be to you. Values are emotionally laden words that represent concepts that we feel deeply about.

One final point about emotions is that we have very little control over them. Our emotions tend to be triggered by external events: images (pictures of starving children, sexy people, beautiful art); incidents (passing or failing an exam, a marriage, a funeral); words (of love, hate, humour and inspiration). Physical actions, such as smiles, hugs, kisses, a slap, tickle or punch, can all trigger emotions.

Interestingly, love could be considered either a value or an emotion. It's an emotion when we are in love, immersed in the uplifting emotion. It's a value when we have an objective experience of it, such as in the concepts 'The world needs love' or parental love. These concepts represent a way of being rather than expressing the emotion of love.

Our emotions therefore seem to arrive and evaporate with little control by us. I refer to this emotional response as living from the outside in, where external events influence and trigger our internal experience of life — our emotions.

By determining and living our values, however, we can create the opposite and potentially balancing effect of living from the inside out. Our values only exist internally. By determining which of these values we choose to emphasise the most, we can deliberately design our external lifestyle and behaviour to be an expression of our values. The end result is that we can live from the inside out.

To do this we must first understand how to live our personal values.

CHAPTER 3

True North values alignment

Behind every fulfilled person
is a set of high-priority values.

Having a clear understanding of your values enables you to be specific about what is important to you in life and then to tailor your life to deliberately experience these things. Too often people find themselves leading lives that are incongruent with their values and their own sense of what is important to them. This leads to unaligned behaviour, which is experienced as procrastination, indecision, anxiety, uncertainty, stress and poor decision-making. A useful metaphor for a life lived in alignment with values is 'True North'. By this I mean having a specific and true sense of direction in our lives, knowing what is most important to us and living our lives accordingly. True North is a metaphor for living your values.

True North is a way of behaving and being that honours your value priorities — it defines who you really are. It is what you are passionate about. It is when you express the best in yourself and when life offers you the greatest returns on your efforts. True North is a journey rather than a specific destination, and it is more about making constant corrections than attaining perfection. True North is a way of living — an end in itself.

True North is about knowing your values and living them. You have experienced True North if you have ever undertaken some endeavour that felt absolutely rewarding and aligned with all you have to offer as a person. You have also experienced True North if you have ever engaged in something that you were happy to do regardless of the pay, time or effort required because you knew in every cell of your body that this was a way of expressing and revealing a part of who you really are.

Finding True North for yourself is to fall in love with life. American philosopher William James wrote: 'I have often thought that the best way to define a man's character would be to seek out the particular attitude in which, when it came upon him, he felt himself most deeply and intensively active and alive. At such times there is a voice inside that speaks and says, "this is the real me".'

Finding your own True North is like finding a sense of your real self. It is an authentic voice, your own voice, not some jaded repetition of society's demands, or the well-meaning and limiting beliefs of people who have influenced you to be something other than who you really are. True North is you at your best.

Where is True North?

True North is, as I have said, a convenient metaphor for describing a way of being. In reality, True North is a genuine compass direction, which, if you were to follow it to its ultimate destination, would lead you to the North Pole. I have not been there myself, although I did once meet a man who had. This man, who I met in a pub in England, shared his story of weeks of incredible effort and persistence to reach the Pole. The description of the journey was riveting, and the other listeners and I were in awe as the quiet-spoken, unassuming man recalled the hardships and conditions he had faced. I asked him what the North Pole itself was like. I was expecting an equally vivid description of the almost mystical destination. He fixed me with a deadpan look and muttered, 'Boring . . . it was the most boring experience I've ever had.' I was incredulous. How could the North Pole possibly be described as boring? I asked him why he had found it so boring, and what specifically was boring about it. His answer was fascinating. 'You've got to understand,' he said, 'there is nothing there. I mean nothing. It's big, it's white and it's cold. With nothing to see or do.'

'You mean a bit like the inside of my kitchen freezer?' quipped someone at our table.

'Yeah, just like that,' said our intrepid traveller, smiling. 'Being there was not as rewarding as getting there.'

I asked him what he meant by that.

'Well,' he said, 'I've got nothing to show for having been to the North Pole. I have no souvenirs, no photos, no . . .'

'No photographs!' gasped a young woman. 'How could you go all the way to the North Pole and not take a photograph? That's crazy!'

'Well,' said the traveller, 'like your friend said, it would have been like taking a photo of the inside of your freezer at home with its light on. All you would see is lots of white.'

I tried to bring the man back to my original question by asking, 'So what was the real reward?'

'The real reward is having travelled there,' he said. 'It takes a special kind of determination to make a journey like that. You have to really want it. You have to overcome all the doubts in your mind. You have to discipline yourself to attempt and achieve all the things you are convinced are beyond your ability, your know-how and your will. Having made a journey like that, you know you can rely on yourself, and, most importantly, trust yourself. Sure, I've got nothing to show on the outside for my efforts, but on the inside — well, on the inside I'm rich in ways I can't fully explain to you, and nothing can ever take that away from me or replace it. It's mine!

'No,' he corrected himself, 'it's me. I found myself on that journey, a self I only dared to hope existed, and by the time I reached the Pole, I had already realised that this was the me I wanted to go home as, to live as, to be.'

I tell this story regularly in workshops or when I am a guest speaker because it captures for me what True North is all about. The gift of being you. You won't necessarily gain any material possessions, awards, fame, wealth or recognition for living True North. You will, however, find yourself.

Magnetic North

Back in the sixth century, Lao Tzu wrote, 'Keeping to the main road is easy, but people love to be sidetracked.'

Experiencing Magnetic North is when you feel sidetracked or even off track, living a life that may be regularly or constantly stressful, meaningless, boring, tiring, difficult or unrewarding and requires excessive effort just to maintain your position. It may even be a simple unrelenting feeling that something is missing in your life, but you are not sure just what. It is a way of living where your effort is increased and yet your return is diminished. As Henry David Thoreau so eloquently put it, 'Many men go fishing all their lives without knowing that it is not fish they are after.'

A life that is heading Magnetic North often lacks a sense of purpose and is not self-rewarding or fulfilling. It is easy to experience Magnetic North by being unaware of or ignoring your values. Magnetic North can also be inadvertently achieved when you misalign your actions with your desired goals; for example, eating, sleeping and exercising ineffectively or inefficiently when you have a goal of getting fit and being healthy. Another example would be protesting violently for peace, or even working long hours when you have a goal of spending more time with your family.

Magnetic North can be incredibly seductive and can seem to have a gravitational pull on you, engaging you in things that may not be in your best interests long term. Unfortunately, if you are not clear about your values, you may not realise this until you are a long way off track. It pays to have the awareness to notice when you are heading Magnetic North.

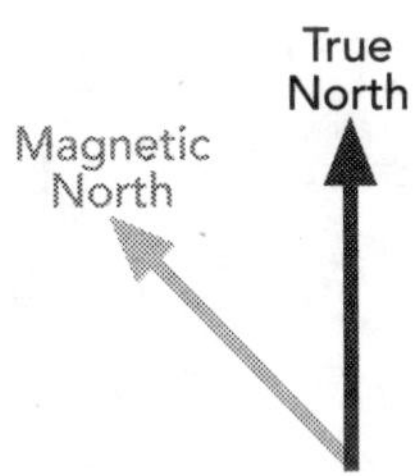

Stephen Covey brilliantly describes the act of following Magnetic North as 'spending your whole life climbing a ladder only to get to the top and realise it's leaning against the wrong wall'. So, the question is, how can we learn to identify whether something is Magnetic North for us? There are two simple ways to do this. One is to clarify what True North is for us, and the second is to pay attention to your experiences. These experiences inevitably teach you what you need to learn.

Where is Magnetic North?

In this book, Magnetic North is a metaphor for being off track in your life. In reality, Magnetic North, were you to follow it to its destination, would lead you to Baffin Island. It is the fifth-largest island in the world and is situated northeast of Canada. I have not been to Baffin Island; however, the Internet provided me with a wealth of information and photos. I found that there is plenty to be excited about and photograph on Baffin Island. You might see narwhal (unicorn of the sea), bowhead and occasionally killer whales, caribou, seals, walrus and polar bears. You can also visit with the local Inuit people and purchase traditional arts and crafts, hear traditional songs and see dances performed. You can go dog-sledding or travel by boat out to a nearby iceberg, chip off some of it and make iceberg tea. You can see spectacular mountain scenery and glaciers. There are migratory birds — the snowgoose and snowy owl — and the island is the nesting home of some 300,000 thick-billed Murres lemmings. There are the arctic fox and the high arctic wolf, and even fossilised dinosaurs. In other words, there are plenty of reasons to want to visit Baffin Island and no shortage of souvenir and photo opportunities.

The suggestion is that most of the attractions for visiting Baffin Island are provided externally by the environment and its people. In a journey to the North Pole the emphasis is on your finding the best in yourself. The difference between the two destinations of the North Pole and Baffin Island and the definitions of True and Magnetic North is the difference between living your values from the inside out (True North) and the outside in (Magnetic North).

In living from the inside out, you deliver your unique and authentic qualities to the world in a manner that shows the outside world who you are on the inside. Living from the outside in occurs when you allow the external values of society at large to be imprinted upon you, while your own values remain hidden inside you somewhere.

I may have painted a fairly miserable description of Magnetic North, and yet it's not as bad as it sounds. In my experience, there is a place worse than Magnetic North, and that is being lost.

Being lost

The best way to explain the experience of being lost is to reverse the wording so it reads Lost Being. This better describes how someone can lose who they are as a person. In other words, they do not know who they really are.

After the desert experience I noted in my journal my definition of being lost: 'the lack of any reference points, including a reason for being somewhere'. At least when you realise you are heading Magnetic North you can make a correction and redirect yourself back toward True North. When you are lost, it often feels as if there is no path. There always is, of course, and you're always standing on it, and it only needs your awareness for the first step to be taken.

A useful exercise to help you make your own distinctions between True North and Magnetic North is to describe for yourself your True North and Magnetic North behaviours, beliefs and actions. For example, you may feel that a Magnetic North behaviour for you is doing something for someone else when your inner feeling is that you would rather not. By contrast, your True North may be to honour the value of self-worth and therefore speak up and explain how you are feeling and why.

Who are you?
Show yourself!

CHAPTER 4

Clarifying your personal values

Your values provide you with the opportunity to stamp your preferences all over your life.

Having developed a sound understanding of what values are and what they are not, the next step, and by far the most important one, is to establish your personal values. This process is exciting and on numerous occasions has proven to be life-changing for individuals because they became really clear about what was most important to them and acted accordingly.

For many of us change can be a disturbing and even unpleasant experience. To put your mind at ease, it is important to note that nothing in this book will lead to any changes unless *you* decide to make them. You are at all times totally in charge of this process, and you will find that there are fascinating and exciting insights in store for you. If you are ready to start the rest of your life, let's get going.

We begin by examining some simple questions so you can explore what your values might be. As you read each question, make a written note of anything that pops into your mind as an answer. (The first thing to come to mind is likely to be a hint as to what is of value to you.)

Determining your values is an insightful process and can take some time to complete. If for some reason you find the process to be laborious or becoming anything less than fascinating, then stop and take a break. Determining your values might at times seem like a challenging exercise. Do not be fooled. Living the next ten years of your life not knowing what is important to you would be challenging. Return to the exercise when you are in a better state of mind.

Remember, values are lifestyle preferences. They are your wants and desires, the things that are important to you. Values are not right or wrong. Don't feel that you cannot write something down because you think it might be silly or unusual or that others might not agree with you. This exercise is about you and your values. You are judge and jury on this matter.

Following the instructions in this book will help you to determine your values in your own words with your own unique meanings. The benefit of determining your values this way is that you can engage in the process with a very intuitive approach. This values elicitation process is simple and can be done anywhere if you have a pen and paper.

Use the following questions as prompts for establishing your values. The questions are provided only as suggestions, so feel free to roam wide and far in your own inquiry and considerations as to what is most important to you.

Questions to stimulate values choices

1. What parts of your life are you most satisfied with?

FAMILY LIFE

2. What are your most prized possessions? Why?

HOUSE

3. What characteristics do you most admire in people (including yourself)?

WILLING TO HELP PEOPLE

4. What are the aspects of your body you appreciate the most?

SLIM FIT BODY

5. What brings you the most joy in life?

FAMILY AND SURFING

6. What do you currently not have in your life that you would appreciate having?

MORE LEISURE TIME

7. What would you least like to lose from your life?

MY HOUSE & FAMILY

8. What would you still like to achieve in your life?

MORE TIME FOR FAMILY

9. What is important to you?

TIME TO DO THINGS

LEISURE ACTIVITY

10. What is important to you that you know you take for granted?

WHERE I LIVE

11. What are your most treasured memories? What would you like your future treasured memories to be?

FAMILY MEMORIES

" "

2 SURFING ...

12. What would you like to have written on your tombstone?

NICE CARING LOVING
MAN

13. What is your philosophy for life?

14. What positive, uplifting, inspiring quotes do you refer to?

LIVE TODAY

15. What makes you feel alive?

surfing

16. How would you prefer your life to be?

MORE surfing LESS
WORK

17. How would you prefer to be?

Now that you're warmed up, you can carry on with the values process. To clarify and chart your values you only need a pad of paper with pages that can be easily torn off or a Post-It® pad, a pen and a quiet place where you can contemplate and write.

Step 1

Write down all your priority values (one value per piece of paper). A priority value is one that has a significant impact on your life; for example, love or health. Although, for example, you might consider peanut-butter sandwiches to be 'nice', no doubt your life would not be noticeably affected by their absence. On the other hand, if values such as love or health were missing from your life, you would almost certainly be affected by their absence.

Some people have difficulty thinking of values initially, so a list is provided of some commonly identified values. There is also the appendix, already mentioned, which contains a list of 125 values. However, focus on what is important to you rather than feeling obliged to copy down some of the values from these lists. Remember, these are only examples, and you want to choose only those that really sing to you.

Some examples of values

- family
- fun
- nourishment
- honesty
- justice
- fulfilment
- loyalty
- synergy
- health
- art
- recreation
- humour
- charity
- curiosity
- honour
- respect
- wealth
- beauty
- music
- acceptance
- forgiveness
- wonder
- independence
- power

- meaning
- authority
- achievement
- sex
- friendship
- wisdom
- privacy
- adventure
- survival
- nature
- simplicity
- God
- reading
- tranquillity
- success
- image
- security
- quality
- benevolence
- travel
- laughter
- sight
- learning
- freedom
- intelligence
- creativity
- ideas

You may write down as many values as you wish; however, try to concentrate on things that are most important to you. If, for example, you were to write something down, yet its absence would not make too much difference to you, then try again and write down something that would make a difference.

Step 2

Note each value's meaning. Beneath each value write down your own personal meaning or definition of the value, like this:

> **Family**
>
> love, caring, sharing, support, Mum, Dad, my spouse, children, aunts, uncles etc.

Repetition in your values

You may have noticed that in writing down your meanings, certain words appeared that you have already written down as values. In other words, you are experiencing some overlap between values and meanings. This is because values belong to larger encompassing groups called clusters.

By understanding value clusters, we can see why some of our meanings and values overlap. A commonly repeated word that appears either as a value name or as a meaning is probably also the name of the larger all-encompassing cluster. An example of a common cluster for most of us is 'security'.

As a means of achieving a sense of security, we may value a number of different things, such as family, friends, home and wealth. When defining these values we may discover that the word 'security' keeps appearing as part of the meaning. This is because it is the value cluster to which all the individual values are a subset. This situation indicates that security should be included as a value in its own right, on its own piece of paper with its own definition. You would also retain the other values of family, friends, home and wealth.

When you have finished writing out all your values and their meanings on pieces of paper, move to the next chapter to learn how to prioritise them.

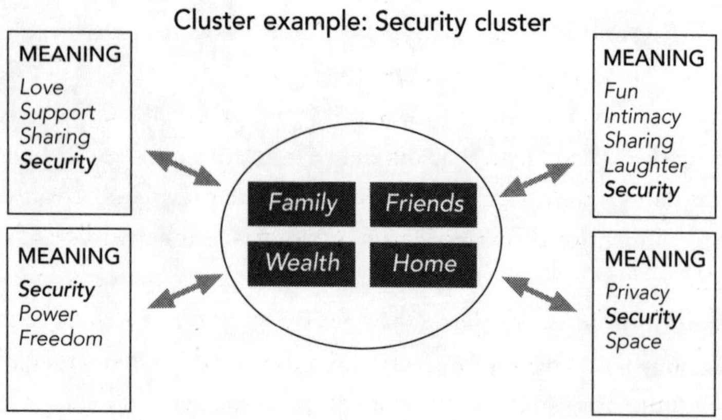

CHAPTER 5

Completing your personal values hierarchy

There is something here that I do not know,
the knowing of which could change everything.

Neale Donald Walsh

I don't believe in living a balanced lifestyle. I much prefer living a prioritised lifestyle. In other words, I spend my time, energy and money on what is most satisfying to me, rather than trying to fit in everything.

Robert Fritz, in his book *The Path of Least Resistance*, wrote this analogy about the role of values: 'One important basic lesson in drawing classes in art schools throughout the world is values studies. The art student creates a drawing in which some objects are darker than others. The difference in relative darkness or lightness defines the space of the objects that are drawn and creates a three dimensional impression on a two dimensional surface. The relationship of dark to light is called the value. There is a lesson here for all of us. We decide what values in our lives will be more prominent or less prominent. We create the hierarchy. We determine how well we will and will not direct our life energy.'

All our values have degrees of importance. So, as much as your work might be important to you, you might decide your health is more important. On the other hand, if you are a workaholic, you might consider your work more important than your health. You might actually fight with the ambulance medics to stay at your desk and finish a report, even as they attempt to get you to the hospital after you suffer a heart attack.

As a warm-up exercise, consider the following four values. Decide which order you would put them in. Use 1 to 4 to indicate their priority to you, 1 being most important, 4 being least important. (Remember, there are no right or wrong answers, only your personal measure of importance.) Write the numbers in the boxes.

FUN	HEALTH	WORK	FAMILY
FAMILY	HEALTH	FUN	WORK

The order in which you have placed the values is a values hierarchy and reflects the measure of importance you place on each one. Consider what your life would be like if you were making life choices based on this hierarchy you have established for yourself. What impact would it make, for example, on quality time with your family? How would it influence your attitude towards work?

Now swap your fourth value with your top value in the box opposite. Review the questions above. What changes do you notice? As you may have seen, the order of priority we place on our values dictates the way we think and view the world. Even though the values are the same, a shift in the hierarchy alters your perception when viewed through your values.

FUN	HEALTH	WORK	FAMILY
WORK	HEALTH	FUN	FAMILY

To order your own values, follow the next step.

Step 1

Write out each of these headings on a slip of paper: Extremely Valued, Very Valued and Valued. Look at each of the values you prepared on slips of paper in the previous chapter and decide which heading they belong under. Arrange your values under the most appropriate heading. For example, if you value your family far more than you do your job, you might place family in Extremely Valued and work in Valued. It is fine to have all your values under the same heading, as long as you genuinely believe that they are all of equal value to you. When you have finished, your first prioritising step might look something like this:

EXAMPLE Prioritised values

EXTREMELY VALUED	VERY VALUED	VALUED
Independence	Health	Work
Family	Friendship	Creativity
Honesty		

Step 2

Create a rough priority order for the values under each of the headings from most important downwards. A rough priority order means you need not spend too much time at this stage deciding if you have got your values in absolutely the right order. So, for example, in the Extremely Valued group you might decide you value honesty more than family. You would rearrange those values then move across to the Very Valued column and repeat the process. Then, having put this list in an approximate priority order, work down through the Valued list.

Step 3

The following step enables you to get down to the specifics and really determine your priorities in life. I suggest you read carefully through this step before you commence the exercise. The process you are about to engage in has picked up the nickname 'the Ruthless Compassion exercise'. It is called this because we have to be ruthlessly clear in deciding which values are really most important to us. It is only through the ruthlessness that we are able to genuinely care for the highest priorities in our lives.

When you have completed approximate hierarchies for all three groupings, look at the first and second values under the Extremely Valued heading. Ask yourself, 'Would I prefer to experience the first value in my life more than the second value?'

Note: You are not actually going to sacrifice or go without the second value; you will, of course, have the opportunity to experience it as well as the first. You are simply determining which of the two you want the most. You are just encouraging yourself to establish a priority.

If the answer is yes, then you know you have these two values in the right order. You would then go on to compare the second value with the third value.

For some people it can be immensely beneficial to make a mental or written note of the gap they believe exists between two values, for example, 'My family is more important to me than my home, and the gap between the two is significant.' In other words, you acknowledge to yourself that your family is far more important than your home. Likewise, the gap between two values might be perceived as so small you can hardly tell the difference. This can be useful to make you feel more comfortable about your prioritising between two values if you find it difficult to choose.

If you don't answer yes, i.e. you decide that value number one is *not* as important as number two, then switch the pieces of paper so the values are in their new positions and repeat the question: 'Would I prefer to experience the first value more than the second value?' If the answer is yes, you can continue down the remaining list. Before you do, once you are past the first two values, just run a quick check through with the same question from the top of your list. Obviously if a value moves up one position, it may influence other values above it.

If the answer is no again, reread the meanings you wrote under the two values to clarify to yourself why they are significant to you. Then repeat the questioning: this process inevitably highlights one as slightly more valued than the other.

Again, bear in mind you will not have to do without the second value! This type of questioning just helps make a greater distinction for you between two value priorities.

Move through the Extremely Valued list until you reach the bottom. Then continue the process by comparing the value situated at the bottom of the Extremely Valued list with that at the top of the Very Valued list. Work your way down the second column and then compare the eventual bottom value of the Very Valued list with the top of the Valued list. Complete the whole exercise by working down the remaining Valued list until you have completed all your values. When you have completed this process, take another break.

Remember, there are no rights and wrongs with values. Whether you answer yes or no is not right or wrong, it is simply your desired preference. The moment you begin to consider or argue whether a value is right or wrong, you are considering the moral or ethical aspect, not the value aspect.

Step 4

When you return to your slips of paper, run through the whole list again just to check you are content with the order. While you are doing so, other values may spring to mind. If this happens, write them down on more slips of paper and insert them into your lists in the places you believe they best fit. If you do add in new values in this manner, be sure to repeat the hierarchy questions again, starting at the top of your list, to ensure your values end up in their appropriate positions.

Valuing Significant Others

I have noticed over years of delivering values workshops that many people have an expectation that significant others in their lives (wife, husband, goldfish, children, dog, Elvis, etc.) should automatically be their number one value. This may in fact not be the case. For me, my marriage is my ninth value. Yes, my wife does know. Currently I am placed seventeenth on her values list. (On hearing me say this in a workshop, one woman called out, much to the merriment of everyone present, 'I'm not surprised you're seventeenth, given the way you think of her!')

There are several reasons why a number of things on my value hierarchy are placed higher than my marriage, including the fact that I valued these things prior to meeting my wife and that this in no way lessens my love for her. These other values are simply an innate part of how I view life with or without my wife. In fact, some of the values that rank higher than my marriage, such as awareness and appreciation, are (according to my wife) the very reasons why she loves me in the first place. In fact, if I had not held them as high values for myself, there is a good chance she would not have agreed to marry me. People are largely attracted to each other through an alignment of values.

If you are happy with the order in which you have now arranged your values, congratulations. Now you can transfer each value and its meaning to the table provided here in the final hierarchical order.

Your vision

Think about what your life would be like if you lived your top five values. How would you see yourself? Describe your imagined life vividly. You can draw a picture, write a poem, cut pictures from magazines and make a montage. This represents your vision of your future when you are living your values.

Your values hierarchy record

VALUE LABEL	MEANING
1	
2	
3	
4	
5	
6	
7	
8	
9	
10	
11	
12	
13	
14	
15	

CHAPTER 6

Living your values

If you're not living your values,
whose values are you living?

Now that you have clarified your values and put them into a prioritised list, the next step is learning how to live them. Because so many of us lead such busy lives, it can be difficult to concentrate on living your life based on all your values. I therefore recommend you begin by concentrating on the top five. I have found most people, once they have completed the hierarchy process, discover they have up to twenty values they consider important. Of these twenty or so values, it is the top five that seem to make the most significant impact on the individual's life.

The first step is to evaluate your current practices relating to the top five values. How are you living, or not living, these values at the moment? It is useful to be aware of your behaviour around your values. How you behave dictates to a large extent whether you are living your values or not. If you are clear about your values and live them you can save yourself wasted time, hard work, and even suffering.

By completing the columns with some key words that capture

for you the essence of when you are living that value (True North) and when you are not (Magnetic North), you will gain insights into how to go about harmonising your life. For example, look at the following table:

EXAMPLE Living your values

VALUE	TRUE NORTH	MAGNETIC NORTH
FAMILY	time together	ignoring
	talking	bickering
	listening	selfishness
	caring	too busy
	sharing	absent
	supporting	

In this example, the number one value happens to be family. The individual, and we'll make it a man on this occasion, has noted that when he is honouring this value, he tends to spend time with his family; he listens, and they talk, care for each other, share and support one another. The individual also identified that when he is not honouring the value of family, he ignores them, they all bicker or argue, he is selfish and even too busy to actually spend time with them.

Use the table opposite to list your top five values and their corresponding True North and Magnetic North behaviours, thoughts, actions or non-actions. Then note what changes you wish to make in your behaviours to stay True North.

Living your values

VALUE	TRUE NORTH	MAGNETIC NORTH	CHANGES I WISH TO MAKE
1			
2			
3			
4			
5			

Well done! You have begun the important process of identifying your personal sense of True North and Magnetic North. These five values will make the most difference in your life. If you honour them and live them you will experience positive differences, and if you ignore them and abuse them you will experience negative differences. As they are so fundamental to you, they are also the essence of what you will wish to nurture in order to make your life meaningful. As fundamentals they are often the easiest to learn and the first to be felt when they are missing from your life. By paying attention to what is True North for you and learning to avoid Magnetic North, you will begin to create a life for yourself that will be more meaningful and congruent with your own primary values.

CHAPTER 7

Your life or your mortgage?

People tell me they can't put a price on their health, while killing themselves to pay off a quarter-million-dollar mortgage.

I once flew from Palmerston North to Auckland during a severe thunderstorm, complete with vibrant, violent lightning flashes and bone-rattling thunder. We were being bounced around by some impressive turbulence. Impressive, that is, if you like that sort of thing, but if you are like me, it was downright terrifying. To add to the overall theatrics, I had just finished reflecting on how lucky we had been in our 50 minutes of flight not to be hit by a bolt of lightning, when lightning struck with an ear-splitting CRACK!

The aircraft, a twin-engine jet of some sort — it had wings and a tail — was thumped to the right and, more worryingly as far as I was concerned, downwards. The passengers as a collective chorus, led by yours truly, yelled noises of a wide variety, each reflecting our varying degrees of shock, surprise, and in my case, unsurpassed terror at feeling the plane dropping so dramatically. The gentleman sitting next to me apparently had direct contact with the higher powers that be, as he immediately registered an inquiry with them as to the nature of our situation.

There was no noticeable or meaningful response to his question, which was unfortunate, as I for one would have felt a lot more secure if there had been. I decided to offer my own humble opinion on the matter. 'I think we were just struck by lightning, mate.'

He looked at me with eyes that seemed to be on the verge of exploding with fear. He grabbed my hand in one of his giant mitts and proceeded to crush it as he attempted in vain to control his rising sense of paranoia. The pilot's voice then came over the intercom in one of those cool and calm tones that implied that this sort of thing happens every day, and quite frankly he had begun to find the whole thing just a tad boring. Although I cannot recall exactly what he said, I can remember that everyone listened intently and no doubt, like me, wished they had actually paid attention to the safety demonstration provided by the crew just prior to takeoff.

'Ladies and gentlemen, as you have probably already realised, we have just been struck by lightning. The is no need to panic, as the good news is there does not appear to be any major damage to the aircraft, apart from the fact that we have lost the use of our port engine.' At this point the pilot paused for what I still maintain was an unnecessarily long time, allowing us each long enough to attempt to decipher the apparent contradiction in his comments about not panicking and only having one engine left. He then continued, 'You will no doubt be pleased to hear that this aircraft is more than capable of making the remainder of the journey safely on the one remaining engine, so I say again, don't panic. Sit back and relax, and we shall have you safely on the ground at Auckland airport in just under ten minutes.'

Of course we all nodded appreciatively at the captain's assurance we would be fine, then checked our watches to see how much of the longest ten minutes we were ever likely to experience had already passed. Then, despite the captain's instructions to the contrary, we panicked.

People screamed, bounced around in their seats, looked horrified and even vomited. The gentleman next to me increased his grip on my hand. The plane was filled with noise and activity, and everyone seemed terrified. Except for one man. Across the aisle from me, a man began to laugh. He laughed quietly at first, and then with increasing volume until he was rocking back and forth in his seat, pounding his hands repeatedly onto his thighs while laughing hysterically.

The plane lurched down and to the right again, and everyone grasped their armrests tightly and gasped in unison. The plane levelled out again. The man across the aisle to my right continued laughing throughout. I leaned across and asked him if he was all right. He looked at me and laughed even harder. I began looking down the aisle for the nearest cabin crew, fearing that the man was about to have a fit, if he hadn't already done so.

'We'll be fine!' I yelled at him across the aisle.

He looked back at me, still laughing.

'What's so funny?' I asked.

He threw his head back in an increased burst of hilarity, and then managed to cough out some words. 'I can't believe it,' he said. 'I've worked so hard for so long. Sacrificed so much, all to pay off my mortgage, which I did yesterday.' He laughed, shaking his head, with tears now pouring down his cheeks. 'And now it seems I'm going to die in a plane crash.'

The plane lurched dramatically again as a deafening smack of thunder exploded right outside as if to emphasise the man's point. 'Unbelievable,' he said, before lapsing back into hysterics.

I found myself beginning to smile along with him. I suddenly remembered I had read a book just a few weeks before that had explained the origins of the word 'mortgage'. The more I reflected on the word, the funnier it became. Thinking my fellow passenger might enjoy the irony, I tapped him on the arm and yelled, 'Do you know what the word "mortgage" means?' He shook his head, still laughing. 'It means "on death terms". "Mort" as in "mortuary" and "gage" as in measurement. It is what you still owe when you die!'

The man howled. It was infectious, and I howled along with him. He would insert snippets of information that just made us convulse all the more, laughing so much it began to hurt my stomach. He said, 'Twenty-five years it took. Always wanted to travel to Egypt, but no — did the sensible thing — put the money towards the mort-gage.' He said the word now as two words, with equal emphasis on 'mort' and 'gage'. 'Wanted to buy a Harley, too . . . and a small fishing boat . . . but no, I put the money towards the mort-gage.' He carried on. 'Wanted to go back to uni and the wife wanted to study art history, but no . . .' I joined him now for the chorus. 'Put the money towards the mort-gage.'

He had suddenly turned angry. Just like that, in an instant, the laughter had transformed into frustration and regret. He burst into real tears, sobbing hard, burying his face in his hands. I sat back in my seat, sobered.

'Wow,' I thought. 'How many of us can relate to that? Postponing what we really want in life in order to be safe and secure, wanting to fit in and be normal?' I looked across at the man, who was inconsolable and mumbling, 'No, no, no.'

Suddenly the plane bumped so hard that we bounced upwards before crashing back down again. I quickly looked out the window to see the flashing lights of fire engines and ambulances racing alongside us. I must have been quite badly shaken, because I remember thinking, 'What are they doing up here?' It was only people cheering and applauding that made me realise we had landed. I looked across at the Mort-gage man. He didn't seem aware that we had landed.

'We're here!' I yelled. 'We made it! We're down!'

He looked up hesitantly through his fingers. 'We made it?' he asked.

'Yeah, we're down, mate, we're OK.'

'I'm not,' he said. 'I own a house in exchange for my life.'

After we were guided off the plane and making our way shakily into the terminal, I overheard the man talking on his cellphone, I presume to his wife. 'I want to sell it, honey! I know, I know, but you wouldn't believe what's just happened. We have to go to Egypt and you have to study art. No, really, we're going to do it.'

He veered off towards the luggage collection, and I missed the rest of the conversation. However, remembering that incident always reminds me not to delay on living my most exciting, inspiring, meaningful values. I'm sure for this man and his wife, owning their own home was really important to them at some stage. However, as we grow and learn and age, our values can shift.

It is important to check in with your values now and then and not let long periods of time pass. It's no use awakening from your habitual patterns to realise, as the plane is going down, that maybe the house is not as important as you used to think it was. Habits can feel comfortable even if they're not — it's the familiarity that's comfortable. On more than one occasion, life has reminded me to pay attention, because forever may be this afternoon.

How to keep track of where your values fit

Whenever we undertake a journey it's a good idea to have some idea of where we want to go and what we would like to achieve. The same applies to undertaking a journey to help you discover your values. To help understand where your values fit in relation to other aspects of yourself, I recommend a wonderful approach developed by the author and teacher Robert Dilts. He looks at values as a series of levels:

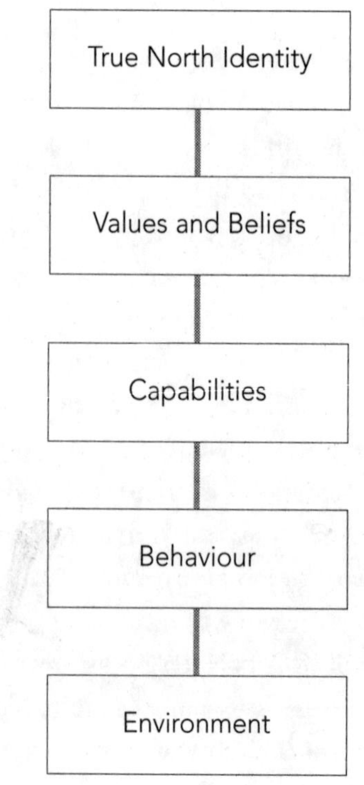

Details about each level are given in the table opposite.

Understanding where your values fit

IDENTITY. WHO are you?

When you are in alignment with your top values, how do you see yourself? What is your role or purpose in life? How would you describe the grandest vision of you at your best?

VALUES AND BELIEFS. WHY are these values most important to you?

What do you value and why? What do you stand for? What do you believe in?

CAPABILITIES. HOW will you be your chosen identity?

What skills do you have to be able to live in alignment with your chosen identity? What skills do you need or want to learn to feel more fulfilled or successful?

BEHAVIOUR. HOW do you need to behave to be your identity and live your values?

How will I transfer my capabilities through my behaviour? How will I communicate my values and my sense of personal identity to others? What behaviours do I want to adopt so I can better align with my values? What behaviours do I want to adjust or stop so I can better align with my values?

ENVIRONMENT. WHERE and WHEN will I live my values?

In what context are my values most valid and important? What are the constraints that might stop me living in alignment with my values? When might that occur?

Adapted from the work of Robert Dilts

By studying this diagram we can begin to see that there are different levels that relate to and impact on our ability to live in alignment with our values. We can also see that clarifying our values can help us gain a better appreciation of who we are and how we see ourselves. We can also begin to see how we might support ourselves to better align with our values by developing certain skills, behaving in specific ways and ensuring we place ourselves in environments that are supportive to our values. By working through these questions and taking appropriate action at each level, you can help yourself to live True North. Each level relates to and supports the level above it.

1. **Identity.**
   Who am I? How do I see myself?

2. **Values and beliefs.**
   Our beliefs are the source of our values. Ask yourself why your top three values are important to you. The answer will indicate what you believe about that value.

   I value . . . because . . .
   I value . . . because . . .
   I value . . . because . . .

3. **Capabilities.**
   What would I need to be capable of living my values?

4. **Behaviour.**
   What would someone see or hear me doing that would tell them I am living my values?

Your identity and values alignment chart

LEVEL	DETAILS AND DESCRIPTIONS
Identity	
Top 3 values and your beliefs about why they are important	1. 2. 3.
Capabilities required to live your values	
Behaviours: What do I need to do to live my values?	
Environment: A. Where and when is it most important to live my values? B. What constraints need to be managed and overcome to live my values?	

5. Where, when and with whom will I live my values?
What might stop me from living my values, and what can I do about it?

CHAPTER 8

Just because it feels good doesn't mean it's good for you

The difficulty in life is the choice.

George Moore

Values are not emotions! So, just because something feels good doesn't mean it is good for you. For example, think of all the things in which humans overindulge, in particular drinking, gambling, eating, sex, smoking. The only reason we overindulge in them is because they feel good. Whether they are in our (or others') best interests in the long term is, however, another matter. The question to ask yourself, then, is not, 'Does this feel good?' but, 'Is what I am doing or thinking of doing aligned with my values?'

As we discussed earlier, Magnetic North has a very powerful effect on us and can provide temptations that seem so compelling, seductive and manageable that we believe we can cope even though it may go against our values. This is especially true when the Magnetic North temptation actually feels good.

Several years ago I attended a lecture given by a fourth-generation Ayurvedic doctor, Dr Gupta, who introduced us to a model of behaviour from the ancient Vedaic texts. Dr Gupta spoke of three predominant emotional states exhibited by human beings: mode of goodness, mode of passion and mode of ignorance. He explained that only one of them worked well in terms of living a healthy, balanced lifestyle that supported longevity.

Mode of Goodness

This is when we are behaving in a manner that is in alignment with our highest sense of who we are and the nature of all life (True North values).

Mode of Passion

This consists of all those behaviours we indulge in when we aren't thinking and are consumed by our base passions. These often override any respect we would normally have for our higher values or what we consider aligned, noble, honest or even spiritual. Dr Gupta spoke of lust leading to extramarital sex as one example, sugar obsessions leading to obesity, and a drive to succeed leading to ill health and stress.

Mode of Ignorance

Dr Gupta pointed out that the Western interpretation of ignorance usually leads to an understanding that something or someone is stupid. Using the Ayurvedic approach, he suggested ignorance is simply the process of ignoring that which you know to be a wiser or more aligned approach. He cited as an example people who smoke, knowing full well that it is detrimental to their health, yet also claiming to value their health.

I could see similarities to the True North model and have developed the following figure to represent and incorporate the Vedaic perspective of there being two Magnetic North influences of which to be mindful.

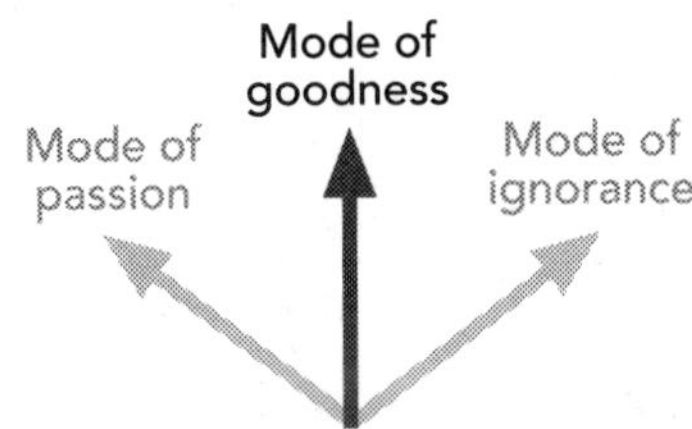

Goodness, passion and ignorance

Aligned Passion

To distinguish having a passion for something from the Ayurvedic version of having your emotions out of control, I refer to passion as aligned passion; that is, as being passionate for something that is aligned with your own values.

Some years ago, my freeform tai chi teacher pointed out that when we do something with passion, it comes to life and can be enjoyed more readily by others and ourselves. Anyone who does something that they are passionate about, that uplifts them, lightens their spirit and brightens them, is heading True North and will often inspire others.

When we do something with passion, we are sharing ourselves with our environment and with others. Think of some of the great artists and scientists, humanitarians and leaders such as Kiri Te Kanawa, Mozart, Mother Teresa, Beethoven, Einstein, Anita Roddick, Gandhi, Martin Luther King and Nelson Mandela. They were or are passionate about their endeavours, and their enthusiasm is easily passed on to others. This caused a celebration of spirit through music, painting, rhetoric or by inspiring social action. You know if something is True North for you if it aligns with your values and you are passionate about it. Passion without alignment is potentially going to lead you in the direction described by Dr Gupta.

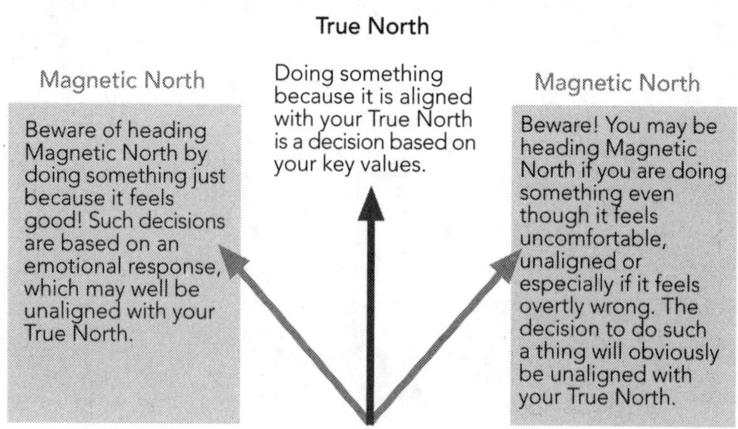

Just because it feels good doesn't mean it is good

Guilty, Your Honour

Another emotional indicator that is worth paying attention to is guilt. When you experience guilt over some thought, action or inaction (i.e. you feel you should have acted), you are probably experiencing a Magnetic North warning.

This feeling, unpleasant as it is, is nevertheless a useful indicator. When you experience guilt, it is almost always a signal to Guide U In Living True North (GUILT). Guilt warns you that you are about to trangress, or have already transgressed against your own values. When you feel guilt, pay attention.

The exception to this rule is when you feel guilt over someone else's values; for instance, you might have been taught a moral stance when you were younger by an adult (at school, home, church, scouts, guides or the like) and, even though you are now an adult and can make up your own mind, you still react with guilt as a habitual response every time you engage in that thought or action. The other possibility is that you are responding to an old value of your own that you no longer value, for instance feeling guilty about eating fatty foods although you no longer value being fit.

To give you a feel for what guilt might be showing you, try filling in this table and see if you can determine which values you might be ignoring.

Guilt and values

WHAT DO YOU FEEL GUILTY ABOUT?	WHAT VALUES ARE BEING IGNORED?
1	
2	
3	

WHAT CAN YOU DO TO RESOLVE THESE CONFLICTS?
1
2
3

CHAPTER 9

From Magnetic North to True North

This is this. This ain't nothing else.

The Deer Hunter

When you first begin to notice you are heading Magnetic North, it is easy to underestimate its influence. Initially you may feel as if you are only a few degrees off True North, and therefore there is no need for concern or immediate adjustment. You believe you can bring yourself back on track at any moment with a simple change of direction, and in most cases this will be true. The difficulty arises when time goes by and you fail to make that initial change. The figure on the next page provides an example of how this might unfold. By the time you finally recognise things are really not working for you, i.e. you are at Point B, you are significantly further away from the path True North than you were when you were at Point A. This requires a greater journey and further commitment to make the trip back.

The gap between Magnetic North and True North applies at any stage of your journey. Even if you have been off track for 30 years, a change of direction now will create an easier journey home than leaving the decision for another ten years.

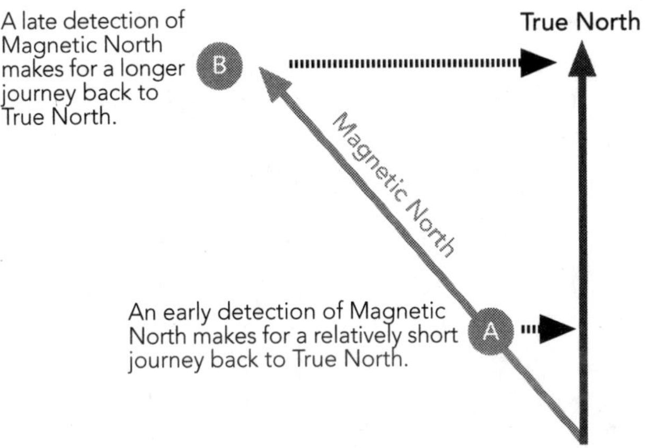

Direction and correction, not perfection

Many people I have coached point out that it must be nearly impossible to live True North constantly and would require a degree of commitment not witnessed since Mother Teresa. But the True North journey is about correction and direction rather than perfection. We need to make small adjustments to our thinking and behaviour to ensure that whenever possible, we are bringing ourselves backs to True North.

We need to be vigilant and aware of some of our own habitual tendencies and old patterns that attempt to distract us from living True North. Staying centred on True North requires discipline, practice and adjustments.

Morihei Uyeshiba, the founder of Aikido, was renowned for his ability to apparently stay centred and maintain his balance even under trying competitive situations. When asked if he ever lost his balance, he replied, 'Yes, all the time, but I regain it so fast that you do not see me lose it.' (A neat trick if you can do it.) Yet to learn to do this just takes practice, patience and a real feeling of where True North is for you.

Greg Louganis, the Olympic diver, describes something similar. 'There is a sweet spot on the diving board that gives you the most lift into the dive. You can't hit it each time. Most times you are too far forward, or too far behind it, too much to the left or the right. The trouble is the judges do not know that, or even care. On each dive you have to rapidly adjust and compensate depending on how you leave the board. You have to learn how to get it right, even when you start from all the wrong places.'

Changing direction from Magnetic North to True North is made easier by discovering the reason you are travelling Magnetic North. What is the purpose of doing so? How is this serving you? Remember, just because it feels good doesn't mean it is good for you. We refer to understanding this underlying motivation as locating our Magnetic North influences.

Magnetic North Influences

Ayurveda encourages a way of living that enhances your health and overall wellbeing. The ancient method of promoting well-being originated in India. Its approach is to determine your body type, body rhythm and body heat tendency, and then you eat, sleep and exercise in a manner that best suits your body type. The emphasis in the East is on maintaining wellness (True North for our bodies), whereas in the West we tend to do whatever we like and indulge in instant gratification until we become unwell, then run off to the doctor for a solution. Ayurveda suggests that by keeping your body in good condition, you are unlikely to become ill in the first place.

> For this is the journey that men make: to find themselves.
> If they fail in this, it doesn't matter much what else they find.
>
> James A Michener

Just as Ayurveda suggests discovering the root cause of our ill health and preventing it from reoccurring by taking appropriate action in advance, so too our values can be premeditated and practised in advance to avoid future regrets.

The next step is to identify the root causes of why you are travelling in the direction you are; for example, if you identified that two of your Magnetic North characteristics are procrastination and laziness, try to identify the Magnetic North influence behind these behaviours.

> The years never teach much that the days never know.
>
> Ralph Waldo Emerson

The influence is the underlying reason why you are behaving this way in the first place. It is the behaviour's root cause. By identifying the root cause and addressing it, you are far more likely to achieve a significant, long-lasting change than if you simply address the symptom. The underlying reason for the examples of Magnetic North behaviours we have just noted might be as follows:

Procrastination — I doubt my ability to make good decisions, perhaps because I have little experience in these types of situations, or I messed up once before. I feel insecure.

Laziness — it is easier to do nothing and not fail. I fear failure.

Try to complete the Magnetic North influence table opposite. It is important to take responsibility for your own actions. So, for example, imagine one of your Magnetic North influences is that you feel you drink too much. Don't blame your friends for inviting you out so often and say that's why you tend to drink too much and wake up with a hangover. Who drank too much and whose hangover is it? It may be that your friends' True North is to socialise, and they manage to do so without getting drunk. You, on the other hand, do not seem able to socialise without getting drunk first. Be aware that other people's True North might be our Magnetic North, and therefore, as the great Bard himself said, 'To thine own self be true'.

As you can imagine, asking a question that will reveal magnetic influence requires some thought and perhaps even courage, because in the process you are revealing what a good friend refers to as 'core vulnerability' — that is, something that we feel vulnerable about or that makes us afraid. Once we are aware of what the vulnerability is, then and only then are we in a position to be true to ourselves and actually address the real issue.

The trick now is to address these influences and underlying issues. There are many ways of doing this, and by reading the rest of this book you might find a number of ideas to help support you in your efforts.

The process I have used to help myself with my own Magnetic North influences is a four-step process as follows (fill in your Magnetic North influences on the tables on pages 95 and 96:

Step 1

Identify a Magnetic North behaviour you wish to change.

Step 2

Ask yourself, 'What is the benefit to me in acting this way?'

Magnetic North Influences

MAGNETIC NORTH INFLUENCE	THE UNDERLYING TRUTH
Example: Stress from doing too much	I am trying to live up to other people's values. I doubt myself.
1 I FEEL INSECURE	
2	
3	
4	
5	

MAGNETIC NORTH BEHAVIOUR	BENEFIT	BENEFIT	BENEFIT	UNDERLYING VALUE
1				
2				
3				
4				
5				

Step 3

Then ask, 'What is the benefit of that benefit?'

Step 4

Keep asking the question until you experience the truth beneath all the deception, and write in your discovery in the space provided, for example: My core vulnerability for experiencing stress might be 'I doubt myself'. I might discover that this is a way of seeking approval from others. The benefit of that might be that I feel internally acknowledged. The underlying value then is 'recognition or acknowledgement'. Knowing this means I can make adjustments in my behaviour, to change from doing too much to asking for acknowledgement and feedback.

I believe the greatest journey you can undertake in life is to cover the distance between you and your full potential. If you are heading Magnetic North in your life and you know it, then change direction now. It pays to be aware that every step you take towards Magnetic North makes your journey longer, because at some stage you will want to come back to True North.

Henry David Thoreau once wrote some inspiring words in relation to any journey undertaken for the liberation of the self: 'What lies before us and what lies behind us are small matters compared to what lies within us, and when we bring what is within out into the world, miracles happen.' By discovering your own internal True North and applying yourself to living it, miracles happen. Your present behaviour, beliefs, values, attitude and skills are taking you somewhere. The question is, where? It's no use crossing your fingers and hoping it is somewhere wonderful, because two years from now or ten years from now you will arrive somewhere. Choose your destination. It doesn't cost anything to change your mind, yet to not do so can cost you everything.

Don't expect it to be easy going. However, accept that the effort will be worth it because the authentic you, the real you, buried beneath these temporary misleading habits, is better and more fulfilling than any influence you have created for yourself. Remember, it is your influence — you created it and therefore it can be addressed. Enjoy the challenge of becoming a better version of you.

Carpenters bend wood;
fletchers bend arrows;
wise men fashion themselves.

Buddha

Never let the things that matter most to you be at the mercy of those that do not

CHAPTER 10

The growth recipe

Growth is life.

Consistent practice of our True North values is the key to personal success. Sometimes we may recognise that although we value something, our current behaviour is not allowing us to experience that value. We need to grow into the value. The secret to growing anything — prize carrots, children, bank accounts, friendship, romance, skills — is the growth recipe. The recipe works like this:

Time + Attention + Quality = Growth,

so:

T + A + Q = Growth

For example, it takes Time to grow carrots. (Time here simply refers to the passing of seconds, minutes, hours, days, months and years.) Because it takes time for carrots to grow, we cannot just plant the seed and then expect prize carrots to appear by morning. We have to wait for the passage of time so nature can do its bit.

We also need to pay Attention. My definition of attention is 'to be actively aware'. Attention must be paid when planting the carrots to ensure they are put in to the earth at the best time of the year, that you place them in the earth appropriately, that you water them and allow them sunlight. If you do not tend to these various things, the carrots might not grow at all.

Finally, consider Quality. Quality is your personal degree of satisfaction or fulfilment as experienced through your senses — what you see, feel, hear, smell and taste — that satisfies you. You would grow the carrots to the size and colour and taste that you wished.

Using the chart that follows, you can make your TAQ assessment for each of your first five values to establish to what extent you are living them in each of the areas. You will immediately determine where more Time, Attention or Quality needs to be focused in order to grow your experience of your values.

One final point. On several occasions people have commented to me that it wasn't so much a case that they had too little time or attention on something, their concern was that they had too much time — for example, they spent too much time with other people when they longed for some privacy. The chart is based on a scale of 1 to 5, with 5 representing the perfect amount of Time, Attention or Quality. In this case I suggest you score yourself less than 5 if you are putting a bit too much time into something and suffering for it. Likewise, score yourself closer to 1 if you are putting far too much attention into something and really feeling the effects.

Completing this process will help you to ensure you are putting appropriate time into your values. For example, if you value your family, spend time with them. Life travels at high speed and children are not young for long. Savour the moments if you value them.

Ensure you are paying attention to what you value. Too many people are physically present while with their loved ones, and yet their attention (being actively aware) is elsewhere.

Finally, ensure the time and attention have quality. If it's supposed to be relaxing, loving and fun, then ensure *you* are relaxed, loving and fun.

All knowledge should be translated into action.

Albert Einstein

Instructions

1. In the table below, write your first five values in the spaces in the left-hand column.
2. Starting with value 1, tick the box in the first row that represents how you feel about the time you currently allocate to that value, with 5 being perfect (you are quite satisfied with the amount of time dedicated to this value), and 1 being unstisfactory (you feel uncomfortable about the time you spend on this value — either far too little, or far too much).
3. Repeat for value 1 by scoring Attention and Quality out of 5.
4. You can then move on to repeat the process for each value.

The following table is an example of what this may look like when completed.

EXAMPLE

TAQ chart

		1	2	3	4	5
FAMILY	Time			✓		
	Attention			✓		
	Quality	✓				
HEALTH	Time				✓	
	Attention				✓	
	Quality			✓		
LEARNING	Time	✓				
	Attention			✓		
	Quality					✓
RELAXATION	Time	✓				
	Attention	✓				
	Quality	✓				
SIMPLICITY	Time					✓
	Attention			✓		
	Quality				✓	

Your TAQ chart

		1	2	3	4	5
VALUE 1	Time					
	Attention					
	Quality					
VALUE 2	Time					
	Attention					
	Quality					
VALUE 3	Time					
	Attention					
	Quality					
VALUE 4	Time					
	Attention					
	Quality					
VALUE 5	Time					
	Attention					
	Quality					

Interpreting the TAQ Chart

When you have completed your TAQ chart, look at your first three values. Notice if any of your values scored three or less in any category. Wherever this is happening, you may be experiencing some stress around this value in your life. The following exercise addresses this situation.

Your Sanity Clause

Your first three values are your 'sanity clause'. Take a look at them. Ask yourself how you would feel if these three values were affected in such a way that they were no longer available to you in your life. What impact would that have on your state of mind? For most people, the result would be catastrophic. If these three values are that important, then it would pay to do whatever it takes to shift the TAQ score as close to five as possible. This recipe for growth has made a big impact on my own life, and people attending my workshops often highlight it as a very useful exercise for taking stock of their lives.

However, having taken stock of our values, we may realise that what we have and what we want are two different things. The following table provides you with some examples to consider, and the table on the next page enables you to define what you have and helps you identify what you want.

How much time, attention and quality do you want? What are some simple steps you can take to achieve these?

You will find that even the most simple action brings about a noticeable and valuable change in your life. Your plan of A–TAQ is the key to living your values. Without taking action, all you have is the talk (a list of your espoused values); when you act on this list you begin the walk (deliberately living your values).

EXAMPLE

Plan of A-TAQ

VALUE	TIME		ATTENTION		QUALITY	
	I Have	*I Want*	*I Have*	*I Want*	*I Have*	*I Want*
FAMILY	8 hours	20 hours	some	more	fair	perfect
HEALTH	3 hours	5–6 hours	little	more	fair	great
LEARNING	4 hours	2 hours	lots	less	great	great
RELAXATION	6 hours	14 hours	lots	less	OK	great
SIMPLICITY	2 hours	always	plenty	less	average	perfect

Your plan of A-TAQ

VALUE	TIME		ATTENTION		QUALITY	
	I Have	*I Want*	*I Have*	*I Want*	*I Have*	*I Want*
1						
2						
3						
4						
5						

Now that you have identified where you want to make changes, read through the following pages which describe some techniques on how to manage your Time, Attention and Quality, then fill in your action plan chart at the end of this chapter.

Managing your time

The most obvious method of managing your time more effectively is to buy a time-management diary or scheduling system from a stationery shop or software supplier. You can also attend time-management courses or read a book about it — ask at your local library.

Most of us have a relationship with time that is uniquely our own. This relationship can vary depending on what we are doing, why we are doing it and where we are doing it. You will have noticed that when you are busy, engaged in something you love doing, you are generally not aware of time. Hence, when you do become aware of it, you are staggered at how quickly time has passed. Alternatively, when you are caught up in the speed of the day's activities and find yourself thinking ahead to what's coming next and where you have to be, you become very conscious of time. You might regularly check your watch and plan ahead in your mind.

These two distinct methods of relating to time can be referred to as being With Time and Without Time, respectively. Understanding the difference between these two and choosing how to operate can give you significant control over your time management in the TAQ process. All of us tend to favour one of these relationships over the other in our lives. However, by being aware of their presence, we can begin to manage ourselves with time and thereby experience a different relationship with time.

With Time

When people are With Time, they feel as if they are in the moment. All of their attention is in the now.

When people are With Time they can tend to be late because they get caught up in what they are doing right here and now, so they forget to consider the future.

Without Time

When people relate to time as Without Time, we do not mean they do not experience time. Being Without Time means people never feel as if they are in the moment, as they tend to be simultaneously half 'here' now, and half 'there' later. They often feel and describe themselves as not having much time.

When people are Without Time, they tend to be easily distracted and often have to get a sense of where they are now by considering where they need to be next. They are able to plan easily and use time planners and diaries effectively.

Your experience of time

By learning to become more aware of how you relate to time, you can begin to adjust your capabilities, thinking and even breathing along with your behaviour in a manner that captures most effectively how you want to experience time. For example, you may find you typically require four hours to complete a task that is not of a high priority to you and you would rather be spending more time with your family. Let's say the low priority task is mowing the lawns. If you don't enjoy mowing the lawns you may find you actually engage in this task with a 'without time' approach. In other words your body is mowing the lawns and yet your mind is thinking about something completely different: a holiday, work, your time with your family, a book you're reading or whatever.

However if you are present and your mind is on the job you are likely to do a better job (thereby avoiding having to go over any areas again because you missed them) and to complete it more quickly. The time you save might then be spent with your family.

Experiment with different thoughts, attitudes and beliefs along with different breathing and moving tempos, to find which combinations serve you best in specific situations to enable you to deliberately choose to be fully present, not thinking about the past or future, or to deliberately think ahead or reflect on past experiences.

Managing Your Attention

Your attention operates in four distinct ways. Try the following simple exercises and notice the distinctions between each.

Attention on others

Take a moment to relax. Now place your attention on something in your environment that is of interest to you. Study it intently until your attention is so focused on it that you have no attention on yourself. When you have achieved this, your attention is on others (you forgot yourself as your attention was fully occupied on something other than you).

Attention on self

Now try the opposite. Place your attention on yourself. Explore how you feel. Focus on what you feel and where you feel it. Focus intently on yourself to the extent that you are no longer aware of your environment. When you have achieved this, your attention is on self.

Choosing how to use your attention

Explore different ways of using your attention. By choosing where and how to use your attention, you can learn to change your experience of life.

In Chapter 7 I recalled an experience I had while aboard an aircraft that had been struck by lightning. Since that experience, as you might imagine, I've tended to be a little nervous when I'm on an aircraft flying through an electrical storm. By learning to control and direct my own attention I have learnt how to manage my experience of my values even in times of some stress. When I subsequently had to fly through another intense electrical storm, in order to direct my attention from one value, 'self preservation', to another higher value (for me), 'relaxation', I shifted my attention from the lightning flashes, crashing thunder and 'significant turbulence' and focused it on my breathing. In a matter of moments I was relaxed.

Simply by shifting my attention from outside to inside my body I was able to determine which value I could experience. Using this technique is like being at the steering wheel of your sense of reality — point it in the direction of your values and use your attention in the most appropriate way to transform your experience of life. You will also make huge changes on your TAQ chart.

Managing quality

Quality is almost impossible to explain. We all experience quality in our lives (even if it is poor quality). The fact that we can experience quality means it must have something to do with our senses — sight, touch, taste, hearing, smell and sound, and even extrasensory awareness. This means that in order to determine the quality of your experience, all you need do is consider what and how you are experiencing it through your senses.

The following outlines cover the various aspects of our sensory experience. By studying these components, we can choose to enhance our experience by intensifying or reducing the nature of our sensory experiences; for example, increasing or reducing lighting, warmth, smells, sound, feelings, contact with the skin and much more.

Read through these lists to explore ways in which you might change the quality of your experience.

Visual components

You can enhance your experience of the quality of your values through enhancing the quality of any of the following:

- colours
- perspective
- showing
- clarity
- watching
- foreseeing
- illustrating
- lighting
- examining
- shining
- revealing
- reflecting
- noticing
- imagining

Sound components

You can enhance your experience of the quality of your values through enhancing the quality of any of the following:

- saying
- silence
- singing
- discussing
- listening
- shouting
- proclaiming
- asking

- accentuating
- chanting
- intoning
- remarking

Touch and feel components

You can enhance your experience of the quality of your values through enhancing the quality of any of the following:

- touching
- feeling
- contrasting
- warming
- tackling
- handling
- smoothing
- acting
- relaxing
- moving
- grasping
- pushing
- pulling
- cleaning
- untangling
- lifting
- running
- holding
- comforting
- sharing
- caring
- empathising
- meditating
- sweetening
- flavouring
- scenting
- tasting
- smelling

Summary

Using any of the techniques outlined here, enhance your experience of your values through better management of your Time, Attention and Quality. Copy the following table five times, so you have one for each of your top five values, and map out how you might better live your values.

Action plan for resolving Time, Attention and Quality conflicts

EXAMPLE

VALUE Family

TIME Apply time management schedule on computer at work, to avoid working late.

ATTENTION Ensure I place my attention on my husband and children when I am with them.

QUALITY Become more involved with my family by increasing the quality of my looking, listening, talking, laughing and sharing.

Your action plan for resolving Time, Attention and Quality conflicts

VALUE

TIME

ATTENTION

QUALITY

CHAPTER 11

Your values and prioritising your lifestyle

Become twice what you are by dropping half of what you're doing. Our values influence what we move towards and away from in life.

I read the following story in the *Clipboard* newsletter written by Dick Hubbard, director of Hubbard's Cereals, although the original source is unknown.

> One day an expert in time management was speaking to a group of business people. To illustrate a point, he used an example the students would never forget. As he stood in front of the group of high-powered overachievers, he said, 'OK, time for a quiz,' and pulled out a two-litre wide-mouthed jar and set it on the table in front of him.
>
> He also produced about a dozen fist-sized rocks and carefully placed them, one at a time, into the jar. When the jar was filled to the top and no more rocks would fit inside, he asked, 'Is this jar full?' Everyone in the class yelled, 'Yes!'
>
> The time-management expert replied, 'Really?' He

reached under the table and pulled out a bucket of gravel. He dumped some gravel in and shook the jar, causing pieces of gravel to work themselves down into the spaces between the bigger rocks. He asked the group once more, 'Is this jar full?' By this time the class was onto him. 'Probably not,' one student answered.

'Good,' the expert replied. He reached under the table and brought out a bucket of sand. He started dumping the sand in the jar and it went into all of the spaces left between the rocks and the gravel. Once again he asked, 'Is this jar full?'

'No!' shouted the class. He grabbed a jug of water and poured it in until the jar was full to the brim. Then he looked at the class and asked, 'What is the point of this illustration?'

One eager person raised his hand and said, 'Because this lesson is about time management, the point is, no matter how full your schedules, if you try really hard you can always fit more into it.'

'No,' the lecturer said, 'That's not the point. The point this illustration teaches us is that if you don't put the big rocks in first, you'll never get them in at all.'

'What are the "big rocks" in your life?' asked the speaker. 'A project you want to accomplish? Time with your loved ones? Your faith, your education, your finances? A cause, teaching or helping others? Remember to sort out the big rocks and put them in first or you'll never get them in at all.'

The same can be said of our values. Ensure you experience the most important values first, because if you don't, the lesser values, although experienced, will still leave you feeling unfulfilled.

> Human existence is a struggle between spirit and matter, in which all too often men attach far more importance to matter than to spirit.
>
> Omraan Mikhaël Aivanhov

There is an interesting formula used in business called the Pareto Principle, or more commonly the 80:20 rule. This law asserts that a specific small amount of effort creates most of the results. For instance, across Australia it has been estimated that in business sales teams, 20 per cent of the salespeople generate 80 per cent of the sales. In other words, one-fifth of all salespeople in Australia are responsible for generating four-fifths of the sales revenue. Similarly, this rule asserts that 20 per cent of a company's client base provides it with 80 per cent of its business.

The principle was discovered by the Italian economist, Vilfredo Pareto (1848–1923), while he was researching patterns of wealth and income in nineteenth-century England. He discovered that most of the wealth of the land went to a minority of the population — maybe things haven't changed so much over the last hundred years. He studied other nations' economic distribution patterns and reviewed historical records of various nations, and found that a pattern was apparent wherever he looked.

Pareto himself did not coin the phrase '80:20' or even arrive at this percentage mixture; others did that after he discovered the pattern. The 80 per cent and 20 per cent shouldn't be taken literally. In simple terms, they refer to the majority and minority, although it can be interesting to work out the approximate percentage for yourself. What he did was to determine that there existed a predictable and unbalanced distribution of wealth. The 80:20 rule is of significance to us and our personal values. If we accept that the minority of our efforts produce the majority of our results, then the connotations for values and lifestyle become quite exciting.

Consider the possibility that 80 per cent of your life's energy and time is probably producing only 20 per cent of your achievements. This means that the vast majority of your efforts contribute only in a small way to your results.

We might also consider happiness in our lives from the same perspective — 80 per cent of your happiness in life has probably come from 20 per cent of your experiences. The value connotation of this phenomenon is that if we value happiness, then huge amounts of our life pass by in what we might describe as low-value experiences.

This may sound a bit depressing at first because it suggests that if you were able to tally up all the important results you have achieved in your life, you would find that a high proportion of them (approximately 80 per cent) come from only a small percentage of your life's efforts (approximately 20 per cent).

This is of particular interest to us from a value perspective for two reasons. If we value results, then it would be prudent to understand which 20 per cent of our efforts generate the 80 per cent of our results. Second, we can then learn to dedicate more of our resources to the action or efforts in our lives that generate the most results and reduce the time and effort we currently invest in areas that are only providing low-value returns. A major benefit of having completed a values hierarchy is that you now know what the top 20 per cent of your values are. It is important to become aware of those parts of your life that are related to your top values and those that are related to the lesser values, and consider this when allocating how you spend your time.

Twice as happy

In the table on the next page, make a list of y
and for each value identify the areas of your
contributed most to you experiencing that value. For exa
the value of wellbeing you might list experiences that have provided you with the greatest degree of wellbeing.

> Beneath the complexity of life lie
> deeper and deeper layers of simplicity.

When you have completed this, consider if there are any common themes emerging from the list that can help you identify how best to increase your experience of all these values. For example, you might discover that an underlying theme contributing to all your positive experiences of each value is spending time engaged in activities you consider challenging; or perhaps it is time spent with people you love; or it could be your career or travel.

This exercise might appear fairly simplistic at first glance; however, I find that people are often able to define specific aspects of life that are particularly valuable to them that are currently hidden beneath the obviousness of the actual activity itself. On more than one occasion this has led to people making significant changes in their lives. It is so easy to claim to have a set of values and yet not actually live them. Just look at most corporate organisations if you need any convincing. So many claim to have values and so few actually practise them. Give it a try and see what happens.

Value-laden experiences

VALUE	LIFE EXPERIENCES CONTRIBUTING TO THIS VALUE
1	
2	
3	
4	
5	

> In every block of marble I see a statue as plain as though it stood before me, shaped and perfect in attitude and action. I have only to hew away the rough walls that imprison the lovely appartion to reveal it to other eyes as mine see it.
>
> Michelangelo

The more aware we are of what is important to us, the easier it is to clarify the activities that provide the greatest return on our life-energy investment. Once we know this, we can direct our time, money, attention, thinking and energy into multiplying our 20 per cent experiences. At the same time we can reduce or even eliminate the low-value areas of our lives.

To do this you need to clarify what you really want and what is important to you — your values. Many of us seem to over-complicate our lives searching for happiness or fulfilment. Clarifying your values, honouring them and living them brings both happiness and fulfilment.

The moment we start to think in terms of 80:20 we become very aware of how much 'stuff' is surplus in our lives. My wife and I experienced this recently when we sorted out our CD collection. On a wet Sunday afternoon we took it upon ourselves to apply the 80:20 rule to our music. We spread out our CDs and whenever we came to a CD that one of us listened to regularly, we put it in a pile that we called 'stay'. The others went into a 'go' pile. When we had finished sorting the two piles we began to count them. My wife counted the 'stay' pile and announced there were 50 CDs in the pile. The 'go' pile had 194 CDs. We then worked out that 20 per cent of the total CDs was 49, just one short of the 50 we had actually put aside to keep.

We took the 194 CDs to which we rarely or infrequently

listened to a second-hand music store and traded them in for just under $700, which we put towards a holiday overseas. The point of the exercise was twofold. We reclaimed nearly $700 worth of low-value music that could be better invested in a higher priority. We also realised we had spent approximately $6000 on the 194 CDs that we listened to infrequently, and which were therefore by definition of lower value to us.

We set about exploring possible common themes of the CDs that comprised our top 20 per cent so that we might purchase CDs more accurately in the future, multiplying our positive experience high-value listening collection. We listed the common themes that emerged:

- uplifting, passionate and moving melody
- meaningful, thought-provoking and positive lyrics
- expansive, spacious instrumental

It came as no surprise that these themes were in total alignment with our own personal top five values. We committed there and then to purchase only CDs that met at least one of our three criteria for our definition of values-based music.

An interesting point to mention, for those of you who think this all sounds a little ruthless, is that five days later I could only recall seven of the 194 CDs we had traded in. That gave me a real indication of how much I did not miss them. Try this exercise yourself (even if you don't believe you would trade in your low-value CDs) simply as an experiment in whether the 80:20 rule relates to your music collection. If you decide to trade in the low-value CDs, you might be surprised at the pleasant feeling you experience by decluttering part of your life.

A few things make the most difference,
and the big things so often are the little things.

My wife and I also have an annual 80:20 inspection of our wardrobe. The end result is a satisfying trip to our local city mission to donate the 80 per cent of our wardrobe that we wear only 20 per cent of the time. It's an immensely liberating experience and also provides you with a wonderful opportunity to understand the types of clothes you typically waste your money on.

Now I am sure there are people who will read this segment and think, 'That is all very well, but I need clothes for special occasions, too.' My experience has been no, you do not. It's amazing what you can get away with wearing when that is all you own. It is also amazing the value your money can provide you with when it is spent on something that is of greater value to you. (If, however, great value for you is wearing an expensive garment once a year, and you are not feeling short of cash in other areas of your life, then you would be best to ignore this concept.)

Check it out for yourself — try it on your wardrobe, check out your shoes, food, books . . . The values expressed in your expenditures may not be the values you want to be living.

Chapter 12

Values and money

You can't waste away in a life of
meaningless jobs, cramming life with trivia.
The supreme insistence of life is that you
enter the adventure of creating yourself.

Brian Swimme

A question often asked about values is about the relationship between values and money. As I stated earlier, money is not a value. What you do with the money, and how it makes you feel and what it represents to you are values. For example, money might provide me with a sense of security, freedom, excitement or even power. It is these feelings that are actually the values, not the money. The money is just a means to attaining a value.

If you are working to get ahead,
pause to consider — ahead of what?

Two of the most helpful books I've read are *Your Money Or Your Life* by Joe Dominguez and Vicki Robin and *Money Drunk, Money*

Sober by Julia Cameron and Mark Bryan. These books are very helpful if you are committed to living a values-based life.

One of the key concepts discussed in these books is that when we begin to understand that we are sacrificing our life units (hours) for a wage, we are also sacrificing our life energy when we purchase something. It therefore makes sense to consider before buying something whether you are prepared not just to spend the money, but whether it is worth the life units you had to invest to earn the money to purchase it. For example, let's say I earned $12 an hour net after tax. I deduct what it costs me to work — train fare or petrol, wardrobe costs and any other necessary investment. Now I want to buy a CD for $35. I ask myself, 'Is this CD really worth three hours of my life energy to earn the money to pay for it?' I have found on numerous occasions that asking this type of question has saved me from spending money on something that is not that important to me anyway.

When in a buying mood, consider, 'What do I have to do to earn the dollars to buy this, and do I really want it anyway?' As *Your Money or Your Life* suggests, 'Twenty-five hours of life energy spent on eating out may seem fine — until you realize upon reflection that you devoted only eight hours this month to one of your children. For many people, the values expressed in their expenditure are not the values they really want to be living.'

Using your list of values and the chart that follows, assign to the various expenditure areas of your life a list of any of your associated values that you believe relate to that particular expenditure. Then consider whether your personal values are aligned with the values associated with your expenditure. In the alignment column assign a rank from 1–5 giving one point for each value you've written down that also appears in your top five. Consider the following example in the table on page 129. If my top five values are, in order of priority, family, health, security, beauty and contemplation, by comparing my expenditures with my top five values, you can see why I have allocated the alignment scores I have selected.

Based upon the results of this chart, you can see I may want to make some adjustments (depending on the amounts involved, of course) to my expenditure on cigarettes (a low priority because only one value, security, is associated with it), car payments (perhaps I could trade down) and clothing (if I am buying to be fashionable, for example). I might, however, want to maintain my expenditures or even increase them in the areas of holidays, food, the mortgage (to pay it off quicker) and the kids' education (maybe start to save for their tertiary education). Try the exercise for yourself using the chart on page 131. Write down any insights or action to be taken as a result of this exercise.

Enough is a feast

I remember that while crossing the Sahara Desert we ran extremely low on food and had to ration our daily intake to two bran crackers and a tablespoon of sauerkraut. This situation lasted for several days, and towards the end of this period we were beginning to feel quite sorry for ourselves as we believed we were really suffering. I remember listening to a conversation between some of my travelling companions one evening around the fire as they talked about the fact that now we really knew exactly what it felt like to experience hunger.

The very next day we drove through a village that was obviously going through a severe drought and was in the grip of a drastic food shortage. We shared what we could with the villagers and got a reality check on what real hunger was all about. It certainly made

Expenditure values alignment assessment

EXAMPLE

EXPENDITURE	ASSOCIATED VALUES	ALIGNMENT SCORE
FOOD	family, health, security, beauty	4
KIDS' SCHOOLING	family, health, security	3
MORTGAGE	family, health, security	3
BOOKS	beauty, contemplation	2
MOVIES/VIDEOS	contemplation	1
CLOTHING	beauty, health	2
INSURANCE, CAR	security	1
FAMILY HOLIDAY	family, health, security, contemplation, beauty	5
CIGARETTES	security	1

Top five values in this example: family, health, security, beauty, contemplation

us view our own situation in a completely different light. No one complained about being hungry after that. I only made one entry in my journal that night: 'Enough is a feast.'

Many of us in privileged countries seem to have forgotten this concept. The effort you have to invest to create money to pay for material goods may not be giving you quite the return you think it is when you consider your values. Making some changes in your expenditures and simplifying your life so it revolves around that which is most important to you will provide increased fulfilment.

Put it in context

Remember, value is what is important to you in a particular context. Values provide the criteria for determining the relative importance of that value. For example the opportunity to work hard for one year and at the year's end be rewarded with a brand new Ferrari may sound like good value, if you value Ferraris. However how do you feel about the same opportunity if I also inform you that working that hard for one year may jeopardise a number of your current friendships, your marriage or even your health? Do you feel differently? Does the Ferrari still represent the same overall value to you?

In marketing terms, the value of a product is determined by the price it costs you to attain the item divided by the experience you can expect to gain from the item. In other words, is the cost worth the experience? What you value in life often changes when you evaluate it from the wider and deeper perspective of your personal values.

Money is not required to buy one necessity of the soul.

Henry David Thoreau

Expenditure values alignment assessment

EXPENDITURE	ASSOCIATED VALUES	ALIGNMENT SCORE
1		
2		
3		
4		
5		
6		
7		
8		
9		
10		

CHAPTER 13

Values-based goal-setting

Preference x Priority = Value

If you have ever experienced difficulty in consistently achieving your goals, you may have set goals that are not aligned with your values. You will therefore lack the necessary motivation to persevere and achieve. Your values are what motivate you to do one thing over another. The more you want something, the more likely you are to engage in activities that satisfy or work towards that value.

Motivation

Your first five values create your current motivation strategy. To help you understand the relationship between your values and your goals, use the table on page 134 to make a brief list of some of your current goals, ambitions or projects. For each goal, consider its relationship to each of your top five values, then ticking the relevant box where there is a positive relationship (i.e. the value supports achieving the goal and vice versa) or put a cross in the box if there is not. Check each goal in relation to all five values.

EXAMPLE

Goals and values alignment

	VALUES					TOTAL
GOALS	Family	Health	Wealth	Recreation	Security	
Travel to Paris	✗	✓	✗	✓	✗	2
Learn piano	✓	✓	✗	✓	✗	3
Run a marathon	✗	✓	✗	✓	✓	3
Pay off mortgage	✓	✓	✓	✗	✓	4
Study for a degree	✗	✗	✗	✗	✓	1

Your goals and values alignment

	VALUES					TOTAL
GOALS	1	2	3	4	5	
1						
2						
3						
4						
5						

When you have done this, use the table on page 136 to evaluate your goals, taking into account the number of values you have positively associated with each one. Although these assessments are somewhat light-hearted and by no means completely accurate, they have over eight years proved to be a valuable indicator of the likelihood of the goal being achieved. If you do not like the way your goals show up in this assessment, do something about it. Remember that you are your own judge and jury when it comes to your values and goals.

Obviously the more values you have associated with a goal, the more motivated you are to achieve it. Whenever you set a goal, remember to check your values as part of the process.

Let your values give birth to your goals

Now that you have considered some of your values in relation to your current goals, you might also like to consider setting some goals that stem from your values. The next process has proved highly effective in enabling people to achieve their values-based goals.

Setting values-based goals

Read through all the instructions before commencing the exercises. You may choose to do this with someone so that they can read the instructions to you.

Step 1 Copy the table on pages 139–40 five times, so you have one copy for each of your top five values. Write in your first value and its meaning in the space provided.

Step 2 Sit somewhere quiet where you will not be disturbed. Close your eyes and imagine yourself in the future when you are

Evaluating goals from a values-alignment perspective

NUMBER OF TICKS	MEANING	CONSIDERATION
5	True North	The goal won't happen overnight, but it will happen. What still needs to be done to achieve this?
4	A-TAQ	You should consider if more T, A or Q is required. Well? Do you need more TAQ?
3	W.I.S.H.	Wondering If Something'll Happen Have you got a plan?
2	Nice try	If the goal still appeals, you're going to have to exert extra effort. Is it worth the effort?
1	A ghost	This goal used to be alive, but now it's probably just haunting you. Can you resurrect this one or is it time to call in the exorcists?
0	You're kidding, right?	Congratulations! You have five really good reasons not to even attempt this goal. Is this really your goal? Just asking.

experiencing this value just the way you would love to experience it in your life. Be specific!

- Notice what the experience looks like. What do you see around you? Who else and what else is with you?
- Notice how you feel. What emotions are you enjoying? What can you touch, feel, taste, smell? How are you moving? How does that feel? Does it make you feel warm, cool, calm, excited?
- What do you hear? Where do those sounds come from? Are people nearby? How clear are their voices? What are they saying? How does it feel to hear those words? What emotions are expressed through their voices? Is there music? Silence? Sounds of nature?
- Notice how you would describe yourself in this experience. What identity are you in? What role are you fulfilling or playing? What is your sense of self? How do you feel in this identity?
- Who else or what else benefits from your being this way? How does it serve others? Capture your overall experience of this value and assimilate it into an all-encompassing experience that you can draw on again at will.

When you are ready, write down your experience of this future vision in the box provided for your sense of the value. Try to use words that best capture your experience. Use positive descriptions, for example, 'I am warm' rather than 'I am not cold'.

Step 3 Take a moment to describe your current experience of the value based on your typical day-to-day life. Note what you would see, feel, hear and do. Note if you can determine any particular identity this appears to be portraying or fulfilling, and who or what benefits.

Step 4 Now compare your current reality descriptions with those of your vision. What differences do you notice? Are the differences great or small? Capture these on the chart in the 'specific steps required' area provided. These are your new goals. You might like to include any new skills or resources you require, or particular behaviours or actions necessary.

Step 5 Note what specific and measurable results will indicate to you that you have achieved your vision for this value.

Important: It doesn't matter if you have never actually experienced your ideal version of the value. Just imagine what it will be like when you do. Your mind will not be concerned about whether the value ideal is real or imagined. If you have ever watched a movie and been emotionally involved with a scene (you cried, laughed, were afraid, excited or sad) then you have experienced this — your brain has watched an image that wasn't real and yet it has let you react emotionally to it as if it were true. Your mind simply wants something to remember and respond to. This in turn enables you to focus more effectively on your vision and channel all your efforts in the True North direction.

You can obviously repeat this process for your four remaining values if you choose. Enjoy crafting your values-based goals, and commit yourself to achieving them. The True North feeling is worth any effort!

Your values into goals chart

STEP 1: Value and its meaning:

STEP 2: Your ideal sense for this value:

See

Feel

Hear

Identity

Benefit

STEP 3: Current experience of this value:

See

Feel

Hear

Identity

Benefit

STEP 4: Specific steps required to move from current experience to ideal experience:

STEP 5: Measurable results of change:

CHAPTER 14

Values and successful decision-making

Unfortunately I have often ended up doing what was in my own best interest after I had explored every other possibility.

One of the most empowering methods for maintaining high self-esteem and living your values is to make decisions for yourself. Victor Frankl, in his powerful book *Man's Search for Meaning*, tells of his experiences and observations in the Auschwitz concentration camp during World War II. He describes how the captive inmates decided how to respond to their environment, and often this choice dictated whether or not they survived. Victor Frankl's insight was that those who had a reason to live, a meaning beyond just themselves, tended to fare better than those who did not.

Making decisions becomes personally empowering when you follow the 'I Do' process. Teachers, philosophers, leaders and visionaries have used this process for centuries — though they wouldn't have called it by this name.

In the I.D.O. process:

I stands for an **Incident** that happens

D represents your **Decision** as to how you wish to react to this

O is the **Outcome** that you experience, which is largely determined by your decision of how you react to the incident rather than the incident itself.

Put simply, the idea is that given any incident life throws at you, you will only be guaranteed to have control over one thing, and that is how you decide to handle it. Your decision will influence your outcome.

An IDO Example

I encountered an interesting situation relating to the IDO process when working with a women's fitness group some years ago. The group was enrolled in a programme to get fit and lose weight. They were provided with a well-designed exercise regime with appropriate food intake guidelines. I had been invited to meet with them because they were experiencing difficulty sticking to their programme.

After I had asked them a few questions, they began to explain that they were still eating foods that were not part of the process, such as chocolate, cake, milkshakes, ice cream, doughnuts and the like. I empathised with them as I had been on a few fitness programmes myself and know they can be a challenge if you do not have a strategy for dealing with a lack of commitment.

I introduced them to the concept of True North and Magnetic North and asked them whether they really wanted to achieve results. They were all emphatically positive in their answer, to which I replied, 'Great, we know you're committed, so here is how it works. Next time you're looking at a delicious piece of cake and it's just screaming at you to be eaten, I want you to ask yourself this question: 'Am I on a diet?', to which you will reply . . .' I trailed off into silence to allow them to answer yes. 'Great!' I said. 'If that's genuinely your answer, you are in luck. Look at this.' I turned and wrote the word Diet vertically on the whiteboard behind me. 'The word diet actually tells you how to rise to the challenges presented.' I wrote more letters next to those already on the board. My final effort looked like this:

Do
I
Eat
This?

They laughed. 'It's a True North decision. You have to commit yourself and decide for yourself from moment to moment that you are on this diet.'

I then asked, 'Who makes that decision?' One woman pointed her finger energetically into her chest and said, 'I do!'

'So if you're staring at that piece of chocolate cake, ask yourself, "Do I Eat This?" What's the answer?'

'No!' they yelled emphatically, enjoying the simplicity of the idea.

One woman commented 'I've never thought of it like that. It looks so simple, and yet I can feel how empowering it will be in that moment of decision. This is going to be great. That cake has had it.'

The others laughed, except for one woman who looked a little sceptical. She fired a question at me.

'OK,' she said, 'that's looks very clever, but what about the exercise stuff? It still doesn't make it any easier to go to my water-aerobics class through the pouring rain and dark after a long day at work.'

She had a point. I immediately had memories of having to

drag myself to training sessions in the pouring rain and muttering my discontent all the way there. I turned and looked at the whiteboard again, hoping the remaining blank space might have an answer. Luck was with me. I walked to the board and wrote out:

Do
I
Exercise
Today?

The rest of the group applauded in delight, but my sceptical friend looked less than impressed. I picked up one of their fitness diaries and pretended to read from it.

'Now, today is Tuesday, so "Do I Exercise Today?"' I ran my finger down the page and said in mock surprise, 'Apparently I do. It says here, water aerobics tonight 6pm.'

I emphasised that the decision was made even easier if I remembered I was on a diet programme and not a self-denial programme.

When the time came to leave, the group stood up, apparently having got what they had come for. The sceptic? Apparently she was the only person not to complete the programme. Just as your first five values form your motivation strategy at any given time, so too do they form your decision-making foundation. Research indicates that our decisions are based more on our values than on rational analysis.

ZEN MASTER: 'What are you looking for?'
STUDENT: 'Enlightenment.'
ZEN MASTER: 'Who is stopping you from being enlightened?
STUDENT: No one.
ZEN MASTER: Then what are you waiting for?

How to make successful decisions

Use the tables opposite to determine how useful your values are in making successful decisions. Before you start, you need to understand a definition of successful and unsuccessful decisions. A successful decision is where the end result or outcome is favourable. An unsuccessful decision is where the end result or outcome is not favourable. Keep these definitions in mind as you complete the tables.

Step 1 Write your top five values in the left margin.

Step 2 In the three boxes along the top of the chart, list three words that represent three successful decisions you have made at any stage of your life. For example, if you are happily married, for decision A you might write Married. For decision B you might write Saving, if you previously decided to commit to saving regularly and you are doing so and are pleased with your progress. For C, if you enjoy your work, you might write Work (representing a successful decision when you chose your career).

Step 3 Now consider the first value and see if the end result of each decision Honoured that value, Dishonoured it or was Neutral in relation to it. Neutral means the value seems unrelated to the decision. Write the appropriate letter in the box to represent your choice, i.e. H, D or N. Repeat the process for all your values in relation to decision A, and then for decisions B and C. To get a balanced perspective, try repeating the whole exercise for three unsuccessful decisions. If you can't think of any, call me and you can borrow some of mine.

Values and decision-making — three successful decisions

Write a key word to represent three successful decisions you have made →	DECISION A			DECISION B			DECISION C		
	H	D	N	H	D	N	H	D	N
VALUE 1									
2									
3									
4									
5									

Values and decision-making — three unsuccessful decisions

Write a key word to represent three unsuccessful decisions you have made →	DECISION A			DECISION B			DECISION C		
	H	D	N	H	D	N	H	D	N
VALUE 1									
2									
3									
4									
5									

Your conclusions on decision-making

Now you have finished, what patterns do you see? Are your successful decisions predominantly honouring your top five values? In other words, are three or more of your values honoured by the decision? This is usually the case when the decisions were based on your top values, even if you were not consciously aware of it while making the decision.

What conclusions can you draw about your values and decision-making?

CHAPTER 15

Personal values and work

To transfer the entirety of life into a unified flow experience, it helps to have faith in a system of meaning that gives purpose to one's being.

Mihaly Csikszentmihalyi

Many of us work in jobs that, given the opportunity (winning Lotto!), we would quit at a moment's notice. This suggests that our work is not in alignment with our deepest values. You can easily determine this point for yourself by asking yourself: 'Would I still do my work if I wasn't getting paid for it?'

A wonderful story I once received by email from a friend (original source unknown) demonstrates the importance of having your personal values clearly defined so as to balance the relationship you have with your work:

> A businessman was at a pier in a coastal village when a small boat with just one fisherman docked. Inside the boat were several yellowfin tuna. The businessman complimented the fisherman on the quality of his fish and asked how long it took to catch them.

The fisherman replied, 'Only a little while.'

The businessman asked, 'Why don't you stay out longer and catch more fish?'

'I've enough to support my family,' the fisherman replied.

The businessman then asked, 'But what do you do with the rest of your time?'

The fisherman said, 'I sleep late, fish a little, play with my children, take a siesta with my wife, and stroll into the village each evening for a wine and to play guitar with my friends. I have a full and busy life.'

The businessman scoffed, 'Listen, I have an MBA, and I could help you. You should spend more time fishing and, with the extra proceeds, you can buy more boats. Eventually you will have your own fleet, and can even expand to control the processing and distribution of the fish. You could move away from this sleepy little village and go to a large city where the trade is conducted.'

'How long would all that take?'

The businessman said, after a moment's thought, 'Fifteen to twenty years, give or take.'

'And then what would I do?' asked the fisherman.

The businessman laughed and said, 'That's the best part. When the time is right, you would become a public company and sell your stock to the public and become very rich. You could make millions.'

'Millions?' clarified the fisherman. 'OK, and then what?'

'Well,' said the businessman with a broad grin, 'then you could retire, move to a small coastal fishing village, sleep late, do a little fishing, take a siesta with your wife and in the evening stroll into town to drink a little wine and play guitar with your friends.'

This story beautifully captures the concept of personal values and how they may well differ from those of other people and be at variance with your work. The lesson, then, is to ensure your values are not conflicted by your work.

Some years ago I delivered a True North values workshop to an organisation. The general manager recognised the importance of ensuring all her staff had the opportunity to clarify their own personal values and be sure that they were doing a job they considered to be appropriate work. She firmly believed that if people aren't happy with their work and themselves, then the company is not likely to see their optimum work rate. (Research suggests she is right.)

The results from the workshop were interesting. Eight people voluntarily handed in their notice within a week of attending the values learning workshop. They recognised for themselves that they were in the wrong jobs and went off to make amends to themselves and their families. You may wonder how the managers at the company felt about this. As one manager put it, 'It's great. Why would I want someone here who didn't really want to be here? How does that help me deliver better support and service to my customers, and how does it help the individual find fulfilment in their work?'

The people who left went on to do some wonderfully exciting things that were far more True North for them than their jobs were. These included playing professional rugby league in Melbourne, becoming a junior professional golfer on the Australian circuit, spending more time with their children during those precious preschool years, sailing with their family around the Pacific, and retiring to coach others and write a book.

On the other hand, the majority of people have stayed at the company and have a strengthened personal reason for being there.

One participant said, 'I've always taken my job for granted. Actually, I probably did worse than that — I used to complain about it a lot. From first thing in the morning, thinking, "Oh no, work again", to cursing the commuting nightmare, to moaning about others' mistakes, that seemed to be a daily pattern. Now that I've clarified my values, I can see that my job is quite literally perfect for me. It's relatively simple, I'm good at it, I enjoy my colleagues' company, the money is fine for what I do and what I need, and it's relatively close to home. It's amazing — once you know what's really important to you, you don't take things for granted any more.' Many other people from True North values workshops have made similar comments and are deliberately and effortlessly enjoying their work more.

Taking your job for granted is quite common. Even assuming that work is not enjoyable is a commonly held belief. In fact, even the word 'work' has negative meanings for many people.

Some interesting results came out of research done by Mihaly Csikszentmihalyi on people's attitudes towards their work. His research showed that people claimed they wished they were doing something other than working, even though the work was fulfilling and meaningful to them. People's motivation at work was low even when they enjoyed what they were doing. Likewise, it was high in times of leisure even though they were actually bored. It seems rather ironic that people prefer to work less and spend more time in leisure pursuits, given the fact that the research indicated people felt more skilful, challenged, happy, strong, creative and satisfied when at work. In their leisure time they often ended up with not much to do and their skills were not being used. They tended to feel sadder, weak, dull and dissatisfied.

Csikszentmihalyi concluded, 'When it comes to work, people do not heed the evidence of their senses. They disregard the quality of immediate experience and base their motivation instead on strongly rooted cultural stereotypes of what work is supposed to be like. They think of it as an imposition, a constraint, an infringement of their freedom, and therefore something to be avoided as much as possible.' He also added that people tend to think of their time at work as time taken away from their lives overall.

What does all this mean? Well, put simply, it appears people enjoy their work far more than they actually realise or acknowledge. By deliberately relating our personal values to our work, we can begin to appreciate how we are actually satisfying and fulfilling things that are important to us in our lives through the actions, challenges and application of our skills in the workplace.

Before we move to the next chapter to look at how we can link our values to our work, it is worthwhile having a quick look at one of Csikszentmihalyi's key points about why even challenges can be enjoyable. He suggests that we cannot enjoy doing the same activity at the same level for a long period of time, as we become bored (see the diagram below). The trick, then, is to balance the level of difficulty presented by the challenges with the necessary skills.

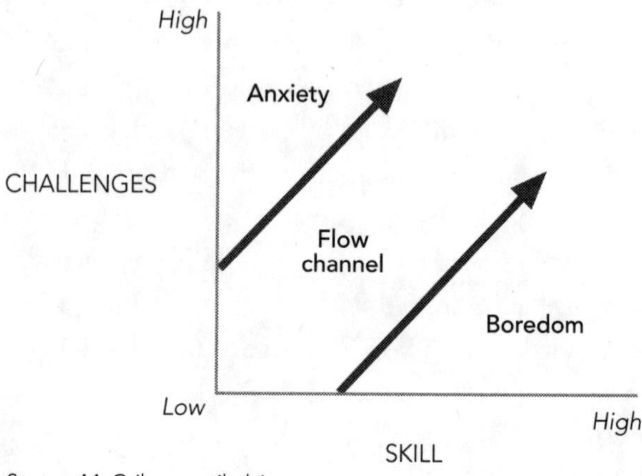

Source: M. Csikszentmihalyi

When we continue to learn and grow by developing the skills and behaviours necessary to meet a higher level of challenges, we achieve what Csikszentmihalyi calls a 'flow experience'. This experience is often referred to in sport as being 'in the zone', and with values, we refer to it as being True North. The diagram has been adapted from *Flow, the Psychology of Happiness* by Mihaly Csikszentmihalyi.

The next step in being able to experience our values at work is to understand how our personal values typically operate in a work environment.

CHAPTER 16

Using your values to value your work

Tell me, Gordon, when does it all end?
How many yachts can you ski behind?
How much is enough?

Bud Fox to Gordon Gekko in *Wall Street*

Many of us spend more time engaged in our work than we do in any other activity in our lives. Unfortunately, I have noticed over the years that many people fail to realise how much they actually value all this time and effort invested in work.

In thousands of workshops I've run with employees, I've noticed that people tend to evaluate this time they invest in their work primarily in terms of the dollars they receive in payment for their efforts. What people seem to overlook is the value of their work in relation to their values.

To illustrate how easy it is to overestimate the importance of money in relation to our values, write how much you earn a week after tax in the space provided:

my weekly take-home amount is $__________

Now ask yourself, is this figure what you are worth?

I have noticed many people on our workshops focus a lot on the relationship between someone's earning potential and their overall worthiness as a person. Do you earn what you are worth?

My suggestion is that no, you do not. Your brain alone is the most sophisticated apparatus in the known universe, so how can a company possibly pay you what your brain is worth on a weekly basis? My point is that you will always be worth infinitely more than what you earn (regardless of your current earning power). If you doubt me, just ask someone who loves you dearly if you are worth the figure you wrote down earlier. Naturally they will consider it a crazy question because money cannot even begin to represent what you are worth to them.

You might argue that of course those people will say you're worth more; it is your boss who needs convincing. This is, of course, exactly my point. Your boss is never going to pay you what you are worth, and nor could he or she afford it.

Therefore you need to consider valuing yourself and your job in a manner that begins to reflect something closer to your true innate value. Look at the table opposite as an example. Imagine you're earning $425 after tax per week from your job. It would be easy to believe that this represents what you are actually worth; but instead of just seeing the money you earn, think about some of the other opportunities work provides you with and what they are worth to you.

When you estimate what each of the components is worth to you and add up the combined values, it might surprise you to find you're earning far more than you realised. Also, if you want to earn more, just add more items to your list (or get another job).

EXAMPLE

The value of work

ITEM	VALUE
MONEY	$425
Satisfaction	$300
Friendship	$700
Learning	$500
WEEKLY VALUE ATTAINED FROM WORK	$1925

Try completing your own list.

The value of my work

ITEM	VALUE
MONEY	
WEEKLY VALUE ATTAINED FROM WORK	

On one workshop, a participant sat back grinning with satisfaction, having completed his chart. When it was his turn to comment on what he had gained from the exercise, he said, 'My wife is going to be thrilled when I get home tonight and tell her from now on I will be earning $300 million a week.' We all laughed, and yet he went on to elaborate: 'In all seriousness, I have never considered what my job is truly worth to me and what I gain from it. I've never seen it as such an all-encompassing opportunity to enrich so many parts of my life. This is really going to make a difference as to how I approach my job from now on' — and it did. I met with the man's employer several weeks after the workshop, and he couldn't believe the difference in him. He noted he was happier, more productive, easier to work with and contributed more with ideas and solutions to daily problems. These had apparently not been strong points previously and he had actually been cautioned on some of them at his last performance appraisal.

This story is not unique by any means. I regularly hear back from management or participants that some remarkable changes have taken place in terms of people's attitudes and appreciation towards their jobs.

CHAPTER 17

Aligning your values with your work

How does your work reflect what's most important to you in life?

As we saw in the previous chapter, one of the most important areas in our lives in which to ensure we are experiencing our values is in our work. For most of us, work is the largest use of our precious time. We typically spend more time each week at work than we do with any other part of our lives other than sleeping.

In order for us to feel comfortable and fulfilled and even succeed in our work, it is important to ensure our personal values are aligned with the values of the organisation for which we work. When I talk about values being 'aligned', I do not mean that they have to be the same. The diagram on the next page, representing a railway track as seen from a bird's-eye view, shows what I mean by aligned values.

Imagine that the rail on the left of the diagram represents your personal values, and the rail on the right represents the values of the organisation for which you work. You can see that both rails are heading in the same direction, enabling the train to rest its

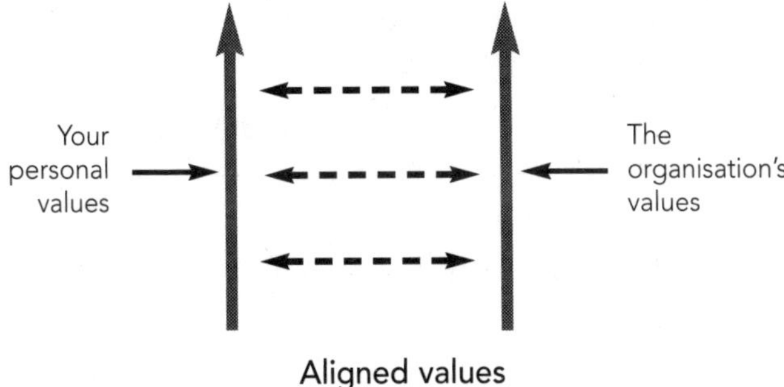

Aligned values

wheels safely on both tracks and move forward without the threat of derailment. In other words, the values are seen as being complementary to one another, and yet they are not the same set of values. Each is separate from the other and has its own unique source.

The arrows between the two rails represent the relationship between the two sets of values; that is, how well your personal values relate to those of the organisation. You will measure this relationship for yourself as a positive or negative experience. The organisation, on the other hand, probably measures the relationship through your performance and the performance of the company as a whole.

For example, imagine your top three personal values are family, security and health and the organisation's top three values are profit, performance and service, as shown in the table on page 161. You can see that the values are obviously not the same. However, if you are able to bring your personal values to work, and in fact this enables you to better support and deliver the company's values, then we can see how both sets can effectively relate to and support one another.

In this example, you can see that an individual has been able to identify how his or her personal values relate in a positive manner to the organisation's values. However, this may not always be the case. Sometimes when you live your personal values, the organisation's values may suffer. This occurs because you believe the company's values are not as important to you as your own, or because of the way the company's values contradict your personal values.

The table on page 162 compares the relationship between the same set of values, only this time it shows what happens when the way an individual chooses to experience his or her personal values means that the organisation's values suffer. We call this situation a 'values conflict'. This means that by living one set of values, another set is ignored or negatively affected. This particular type of values conflict is very common because people tend to live their personal values ahead of the organisation's values. This is especially true if the company has not supported its people in establishing their personal values.

There is a saying my colleagues and I use that captures this point: 'Companies do not live their values, people do.' What this means is that companies are made up of people, and it is these people who live the organisation's values, not the company itself. If those people cannot see the benefit of the company values to them personally then they will tend to live their personal values in preference to the company values. If people cannot align their personal values to those of the organisation, they are most likely (although not always) to live their own values first. This is why it is important for organisations to support their people in clarifying their personal values as a way of enabling them to evaluate the company's values and make it easier for people to align their personal values to those of the company.

You can see from the previous table that your personal values might lead you to behave in a way that lets down or overrides the

Personal values aligned with the company's values

YOUR VALUES	RELATIONSHIP	THE COMPANY'S VALUES
FAMILY	I am able to support my family by helping the organisation be profitable. If it loses money, I could lose my job. Impact on company value: My work contributes to the company being profitable.	**PROFIT**
SECURITY	My job is more secure when the company and I perform well. Impact on company value: My efforts contribute to my department's performance and that of the company overall.	**PERFORMANCE**
HEALTH	I tend to be less stressed when we deliver great customer service. Impact on company value: My relaxed 'can do' attitude helps to deliver high levels of customer service.	**SERVICE**

When personal values conflict with company values

YOUR VALUES	RELATIONSHIP	THE COMPANY'S VALUES
FAMILY	I prefer to take time off and be late to work and early to leave to spend more time with my family. Impact on company value: The company is paying me for work I do not actually do. This impacts negatively on its profit.	**PROFIT**
SECURITY	I prefer to talk with other about the challenges in my work and how they are affecting me. Impact on company value: Generally this is a good thing as it enables me and my colleagues to find better ways of doing things that are less stressful to me. However, sometimes the talking becomes complaining, and if this is done in long discussions, it might affect my productivity.	**PERFORMANCE**
HEALTH	I avoid any stressful situations; for example, grumpy customers or complaints. Impact on company value: Sometimes I may not deliver the best level of customer service because I am trying to avoid the issues.	**SERVICE**

company values. However, the opposite can also happen, when you are so determined to live the company values (in order to make a good impression or get a promotion) that you neglect your personal values. When this happens, the relationship between the two sets of values changes considerably as shown in the example on page 165.

Finally, we may find that both sets of values are in conflict. More often than not this indicates that you may be working in the wrong department or company, or that you might need to look at how you experience each of the values to see if any changes can be made in your personal or work behaviour. If you feel you might be in this position, consider asking your boss, values coach or the human resources department for some time to discuss this situation and see if there are any solutions to the values conflict you are experiencing. Remember, it is acceptable to realise that a job is not right for you. By leaving to find a job that is more aligned with your personal values, you will help everyone. If your company is really honest, they do not want you working for them if you do not find the work fulfilling and are not motivated to give your best effort. Many people we have supported in clarifying their values have eventually left their jobs for something more in line with their values.

Take time to consider your values in relation to those of your organisation. Using the table that appears on pages 166 and 167, write your top values in the left-hand column and the company values in the right-hand column. Use the middle column to describe the experience of the combination of your values and those of the company. If you don't know your company's values, ask. If the company does not have any articulated values, write down what you consider to be the company's top three priorities.

You can now summarise the situation you are currently

experiencing in the tables on pages 168 to 170. The first table shows how you can determine if your values are well aligned with those of your company. Consider to what extent you are currently living your personal values, as indicated by where you believe you would position yourself on the horizontal axis. If you know what your values are and are living them, then you will be to the far right of the axis, measuring a high degree of values fulfilment. If you know your values and are not living them, then you will be to the left side of the horizontal axis, indicating a low degree of values fulfilment.

Likewise, if you are living the organisation's values, you would score on the high end of the vertical axis. This is usually shown by a high level of performance. By considering the relationship between your personal values and those of the organisation, you can determine which of the four possible combinations you are currently experiencing.

Having studied this table and considered your own situation, use the next table and write in the box that best matches your current situation. Describe how the relationship of the two values sets works — how they are lived or not lived, how they affect your experience or your performance.

Having completed this table, if you believe that the situation is not to your liking, you might want to complete the final tables in this chapter to help you identify ways in which you might be able to improve the current situation by developing new skills — for example, learning some stress management techniques to enable you to better experience the value of health. You might also change some of your behaviours to improve your experience or performance of a value. If you need support with determining suitable skills and behaviours, ask a colleague, a manager, friend or family member for their ideas.

EXAMPLE

When company values conflict with personal values

YOUR VALUES	RELATIONSHIP	THE COMPANY'S VALUES
FAMILY	I feel obliged to stay late at work to make a good impression on the boss and fit in with everyone else. Impact on personal value: I arrive home later every day and miss spending time with the kids or being able to put them to bed.	**PROFIT**
SECURITY	I feel obliged to work harder than I want to. Impact on personal value: I am too busy to make friends at work and the company is not paying me for the additional work I do.	**PERFORMANCE**
HEALTH	I have to be so conscientious and polite to customers all the time and always go the extra mile. Impact on personal value: I suppress my real feelings, which means I get all wound up inside. I feel like I am overworking and it is exhausting me.	**SERVICE**

Alignment of your values to the company's values

YOUR VALUES	RELATIONSHIP	THE COMPANY'S VALUES
1	Impact on personal view Impact on company view	1
2	Impact on personal view Impact on company view	2
3	Impact on personal view Impact on company view	3

Your values situation at work — general

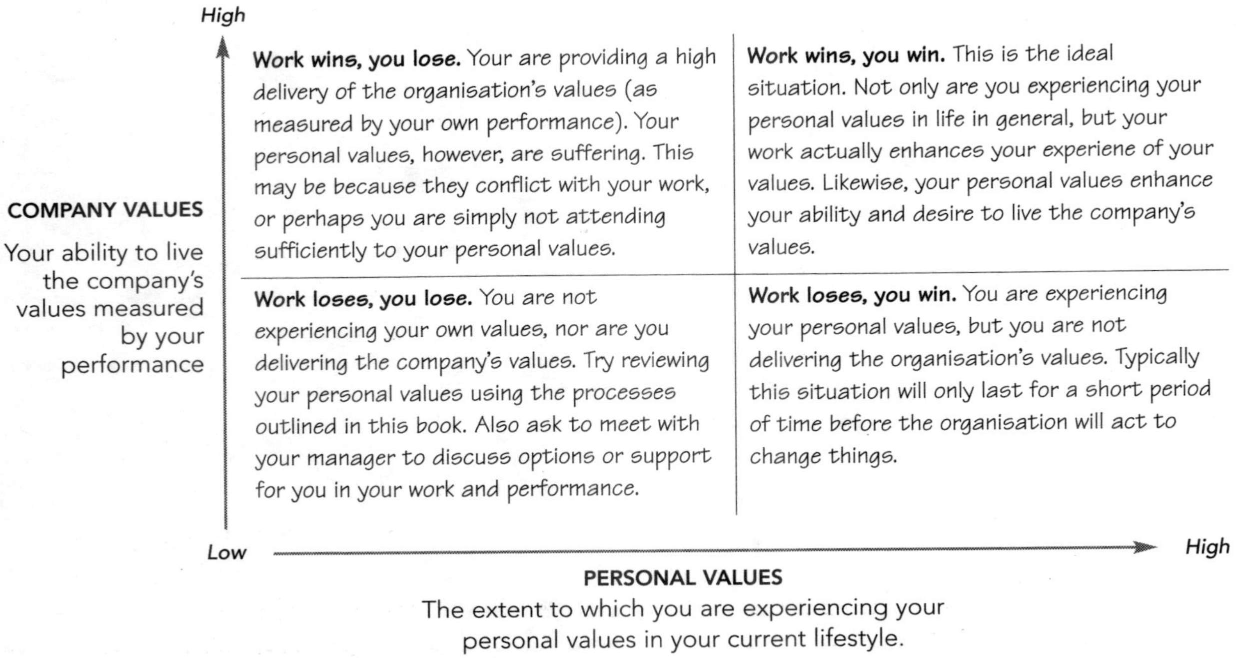

High

COMPANY VALUES

Your ability to live the company's values measured by your performance

Work wins, you lose. Your are providing a high delivery of the organisation's values (as measured by your own performance). Your personal values, however, are suffering. This may be because they conflict with your work, or perhaps you are simply not attending sufficiently to your personal values.	**Work wins, you win.** This is the ideal situation. Not only are you experiencing your personal values in life in general, but your work actually enhances your experiene of your values. Likewise, your personal values enhance your ability and desire to live the company's values.
Work loses, you lose. You are not experiencing your own values, nor are you delivering the company's values. Try reviewing your personal values using the processes outlined in this book. Also ask to meet with your manager to discuss options or support for you in your work and performance.	**Work loses, you win.** You are experiencing your personal values, but you are not delivering the organisation's values. Typically this situation will only last for a short period of time before the organisation will act to change things.

Low — *High*

PERSONAL VALUES

The extent to which you are experiencing your personal values in your current lifestyle.

Your values situation at work

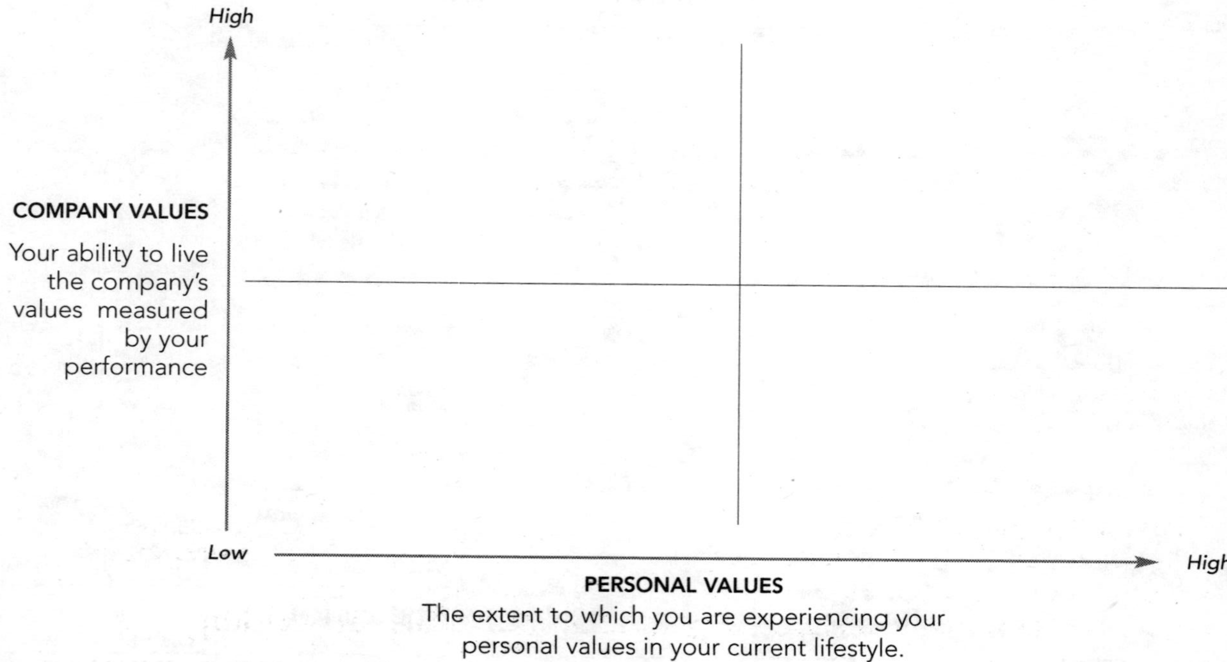

Improving my experience of the company's values

THE COMPANY'S VALUES	THE VALUE'S MEANING	CURRENT SITUATION	SOLUTION: action, skills, behaviour
1			
2			
3			
4			
5			

Improving my experience of my personal values at work

MY VALUE	THE VALUE'S MEANING	CURRENT SITUATION	SOLUTION: action, skills, behaviour
1			
2			
3			
4			
5			

CHAPTER 18

Your values and self-esteem

May you live all the days of your life.

Jonathan Swift

The root word for values is valour, from the Latin, meaning strength. When you live your values, you literally create inner strength. You trust yourself more, appreciate yourself more and value yourself more.

Here is a simple exercise to help determine your current self-esteem. Pick a number between 1 and 10 to represent your current self-esteem, 10 being deliriously happy to be you, to the extent you feel sorry for everyone else who isn't you, and 1 being where you wish you were anyone else because being you is so awful you just can't stand it.

Now, would you like to have a higher number than the one you have allocated to yourself? If so, why didn't you give yourself a higher number?

Remember, you are measuring your self-esteem, self being I, esteem meaning worth, regard or value. Your self-esteem is the regard you have for yourself. Why wouldn't you choose a higher number? When I ask people this they usually respond, 'I know I can do better', or 'I'll feel better about myself when I've achieved my goals', or 'I'll feel more positively about myself when I've stopped smoking and lost 5 kg in weight.'

When we make statements like this we are confusing self-esteem with achieving goals and outcomes. Those goals are all good, yet they have nothing to do with self-esteem. Self-esteem is about self-worth, or, in other words, asking yourself if you are you worthy of achieving these things in the first place. It is not outcome-dependent. It is not reliant on your doing anything! It is only dependent on you valuing your own being.

For example, if you have deliberately lowered your self-esteem score because you have yet to lose 5kg, the self-esteem question is, 'Do you deserve to lose 5kg?' The answer is, of course, emphatically 'yes'. That means your self-esteem could be a 10 if only you credited yourself with the worth you deserve. Don't fail yourself. Give yourself a 10 for self-esteem and act that way. The world needs you at your best, not at mediocre or pitiful, so credit yourself as worthy and get on with creating a wonderful passion-filled life for yourself.

I once heard General Schwarzkopf speak at a convention. He said he asked a commanding officer in the Pentagon if he had any advice to give on leadership. The commanding officer told Schwarzkopf, 'That's easy. Number one, take charge, and number two, do the right thing!' Simple? My suggestion is to apply that philosophy to yourself and your self-esteem.

1. Take charge of it
2. Do the right thing (hint: give yourself a 10).

High self-esteem can be confused with arrogance. I am not advocating arrogance. Arrogance is all about raising oneself above others. I am talking about lifting yourself to your rightful position within yourself — to be yourself.

Your self-esteem could be compared with the sails on a ship. The higher the sails are hoisted, the more wind they can catch to power the boat on its way. It's your boat, so you are the captain and can decide how high to hoist your self-esteem.

Often the level of self-esteem you allocate to yourself can be reflected, heard and noted in the manner in which you speak to yourself. What is your self-talk when you have made a mistake or are disappointed with your efforts? Reflect for a moment on the typical words you would say to yourself in these kinds of situations. If you cannot think of any at the moment, pay attention to this the next time you find yourself in this type of situation. I have a saying I use for myself when I notice I am passing negative judgements on myself: 'That's a loaded belief system you're thinking with, Michael, so be careful where you point it!' This reminds me not to give myself an unnecessarily difficult time.

Compare this language to how you talk to a dear friend or a family member whom you love deeply. What do you notice about the manner in which you talk to yourself (either inside or outside your head) compared to how you communicate to others? Are you tougher on yourself than you are on others? Do you offer others more compassion, support, kind words of advice and hope? How would you respond if you spoke to yourself in the same manner you speak to others? Why should there be any difference? Lighten up if you find you are being too harsh on yourself and especially if this manifests as low self-esteem.

CHAPTER 19

The values of others

We tend to judge others when we underestimate ourselves.

Once you develop a values set and begin to live it as a habit, you begin to create a particular way of viewing the world. I refer to this world-view as being our position of influence. This means that whatever position you hold about a set of values will influence how you see the world around you.

Positions of Influence

A position of influence is simply the position you happen to be in at any given moment. This position holds your beliefs, values, past and present habits, your capabilities and behaviours. This position influences the way you view, judge and behave in the world. Each person holds a unique position of influence comprised of who they are in that moment. Your view of the world from this position is fixed as long as you remain in this position. Only by shifting your position can you see another perspective. The following figure demonstrates the concept by indicating how four different positions can easily create four different interpretations of the same symbol.

The four positions are marked with the letters A, B, C and D. The symbol at the centre is represented by the number 3 . . . or at least that's the way it appears from Position A.

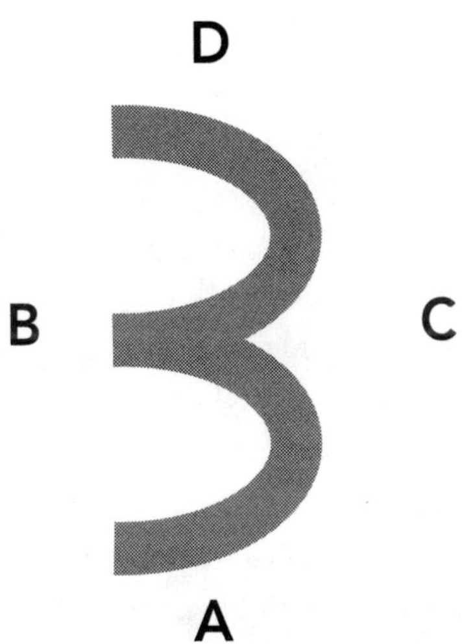

From Position A the symbol looks like the number 3.
From Position B the symbol looks more like the letter M.
From Position C the symbol looks like the letter W.
From Position D the symbol looks like the letter E.

We can now see how easy it is for someone at Position A to think someone at Position B, C or D is quite mistaken if they claim the symbol to be something other than the number 3. If all parties were to debate the point strongly, it could become an argument and ill feeling could develop among those present.

St Augustine once said, 'In order to be understood, first seek to understand.' In other words, before launching into a full-scale attack claiming you are right and the others are obviously wrong, take a short walk around the circle and view the situation from the other side. This diagram helps us to remember that what we consider to be a reasonable view of a situation is little more than a limited view of the whole. You may find this helps you to understand why others value things differently from you.

Likewise, if you were to invite those at Positions B, C and D to look at the symbol from your position, you might find they begin to understand why you hold the perspective you do. They may not agree with you, or you with them, yet you could all reach an understanding and appreciation of each other's positions. Then again, you might totally agree with them or drop your own beliefs in realisation of your prejudgement of their situation.

As discussed throughout this book, the major components that fix us in our particular position are our values. These are influential only because we believe them to be true, and we have adopted them as our own. We believe our position to be the only correct one and therefore consider all others to be wrong. If we are really passionate about our chosen position, we will argue with someone in order to defend it, when that's all it is — a chosen position. The other person has chosen another position. Yet although we claim to have had an argument with someone, it appears more accurate to say that we argue *against* them or their position, and not *with* them as we propose.

As an experiment, the next time you find yourself in a conversation, discussion, debate or argument, do as St Augustine suggests, and place more attention on understanding the other's position of influence. See what you learn and what value this awareness has for you beyond simply winning the debate or proving the other person wrong.

Typically this provides us with an opportunity to begin to

understand what another person values and maybe even why they believe it to be so important. If we are willing to be a little more flexible in our approach to how we interact with others, these situations can be a wonderful source of learning. In particular, the other person will often unwittingly reflect back to us what is being projected from our own fixed position that we are not necessarily aware of. This whole process is made easier if you deliberately decide to avoid taking offence at what the other person is saying and concentrate on learning about them.

> If we read the secret history of our enemies,
> we should find in each man's life sorrow and
> suffering enough to disarm all hostility.
>
> Longfellow

CHAPTER 20

The trail of a true being

It pays to remember when the going is tough that the most important and rewarding journey in life is to cover the distance between you and your full magnificent potential.

One of my favourite movies is Kevin Costner's *Dances With Wolves*. The story is about an American soldier in the American Civil War who sets off on an adventure into the Great Plains. It is a story of self-discovery and the trials and questions encountered. The lead character, Lieutenant Dunbar, befriends a Sioux medicine man called Kicking Bird. Kicking Bird notices that Dunbar is slowly settling into a lifestyle that integrates the best from his past with his learning from the Sioux. One day while sitting by a fire, Kicking Bird comments, 'I was just thinking that of all the trails in this life, there is one that matters most. It is the trail of a true being. I think you are on this trail, and it is good to see.' This is how I would encourage you to view True North — the trail of a true being.

Establishing your True North by defining your values is a significant step. It is the moment when you clarify what really is important to you. It is an opportunity for you to recognise and accept who you are and to know that nothing less than living this to the fullest will do. You are worthy of living your values and enriching your life.

True North

Let us stay true to our course.
It is so easy to become lost,
simply by straying.

Far better to use our energy
to stay on track,
to stay True North.

Here is a simple truth
and a way home.
Make measurable progress
in reasonable time.

All that is required
is a steady grip on the wheel,
a little faith,
a little courage,
and a sense of purpose.

So come on home,
you are long overdue
and dearly missed.

APPENDIX

A values inventory: definitions of 125 values

The following list of values is based on over thirty years of values research.

The inventory started with the work of Paulo Freire and Ivan Illich in Brazil, who used energy-laden words to raise people's awareness of their social situation and to increase their level of literacy. Brian Hall, working alongside them, realised these energy-laden words were indicators of people's value priorities. The concept of a values inventory was born.

Brian Hall and Benjamin Tonna collaborated to develop the Hall-Tonna Inventory of Values. In 1988, Paul Chippendale brought the inventory to Australia. Since then, the process of values analysis has been developed and refined and includes some of the latest thinking around the brain and people's thinking.

If you choose to refer to these values you may find words you have not come across before such as 'ecority' or 'minessence'. These are in fact newly developed words to capture concepts people value but did not have a specific word for. For example, 'minessence' means 'to miniaturise and simplify complex ideas or technology into concrete and practical applications for the purpose of creatively impacting on the world-view of the user'.

Depending on what culture you are from you may tend to view some of these values as needs more than values, which is fine.

Accountability/Ethics

To hold yourself and others accountable to a code of ethics derived from your values. To address the appropriateness of your behaviour in relation to your values.

Achievement

To accomplish something noteworthy and admirable in your work, education, or your life in general.

Adaptability/Flexibility

To adjust yourself readily to changing conditions and to remain flexible during ongoing processes.

Administration/Control

To be in command. To exercise specific administrative functions and tasks in a business or institution, such as finance or recruitment.

Affection

To express fondness or devotion through physical touch.

Art/Beauty

To experience intense mental pleasure through observing that which is aesthetically appealing in either natural or human creations.

Assertion/Directedness

To put yourself forward boldly regarding a personal line of thought or action.

Being Liked

To experience friendly feelings from your peers.

Being Self

The desire to know the truth about yourself and the world around you. This includes seeking an objective awareness of your personal strengths and limitations. The desire to be yourself in all situations.

Care/Nurture

To be physically and emotionally supported by family and friends throughout your life and to value the same from others.

Collaboration/Subsidiarity

Interdependent co-operation with all levels of management, ensuring full and appropriate delegation of responsibility takes place.

Communications/Information

The effective and efficient flow of ideas and factual information to persons in all or part of an organisation.

Community/Personalist

To have sufficient depth and quality of commitment to a group, its members and its purpose, so that independent creativity and interdependent cooperation will be maximised simultaneously.

Community/Supportive

The desire to have, or to create, a group of peers for the purpose of ongoing mutual support and the creative enhancement of each other.

Competence/Confidence

To experience the realistic and objective confidence that you have the skills to achieve in the world of work and to feel that your skills are making a positive contribution.

Competition

To be energised by a sense of rivalry, to be first or most respected in a given arena, e.g. sports, education or work.

Congruence

To experience and express your feelings and thoughts in such a way that what you communicate externally to others is the same as what you experience internally.

Construction/New Order

To initiate and to develop a new form of institution or organisation for the purpose of creatively enhancing society.

Contemplation/Asceticism

The self-discipline and art of meditative reflection that prepares you for intimacy with others and that gives you a sense of being part of something bigger than yourself.

Control/Order/Discipline

To control people and/or things according to prescribed rules so as to maintain the accepted level of discipline and order.

Convivial Technology

The application of technology for the benefit of both humanity and the planet.

Co-operation/Complementarity

To work cooperatively in a group so that the unique skills and qualities of one individual supplement, support and enhance the skills and qualities of the others in the group.

Corporation/New Order

The innovative design of new organisational or institutional forms which, if implemented, would creatively enhance society.

Courtesy/Hospitality

To treat others, and be treated by them, in a polite, respectful, friendly and generous manner.

Creativity/Ideation

Original thought and expression that converts, for the first time, new ideas, images or concepts into practical and concrete forms.

Criteria/Rationality

To think logically and reasonably using a formal framework for analysis. To exercise reason before emotion.

Decision/Initiation

To take personal responsibility for beginning a creative course of action. To act on your conscience without external prompting.

Design/Pattern/Order

To have an awareness of the natural arrangement of things. To use this awareness to create new arrangements through the application of the arts, ideas or technology, e.g. architecture.

Detachment/Solitude

Regular discipline of non-attachment to external things that leads to the potential to live more fully.

Detachment/Transcendence

Spiritual discipline and detachment so as to experience a global and visionary perspective through a feeling of being in touch with some ultimate source of wisdom.

Dexterity/Co-ordination

Sufficient harmonious interaction of your mental and physical functions to perform basic instrumental tasks, e.g. following a knitting pattern to knit a jersey.

Discernment/Communal

To make consensus decisions, relative to long-term planning for a group or organisation, through prayerful reflection and honest interaction.

Duty/Obligation

To closely follow established customs and regulations out of dedication to your peers and a sense of responsibility to institutional codes.

Economics/Profit

To accumulate physical wealth in order to be secure and respected.

Economics/Success

To attain favourable and prosperous financial results in business through effective control and efficient management of resources.

Ecority/Aesthetics

The personal, organisational or conceptual influence to enable persons to take authority for the created order of the world and to enhance its beauty and balance through creative technology in ways that have worldwide influence.

Education/Certification

To value completing a formally prescribed course of learning and to receive a certificate of accomplishment.

Education/Knowledge/Insight

To experience ongoing learning as a means of gaining new facts, truths and principles, motivated by the reward of a new understanding gained through insight. To enjoy the 'Aha' experience of learning.

Efficiency/Planning

To plan processes and activities which, when implemented, will make the best possible use of available resources.

Empathy

The ability of being able to see things from other people's point of view.

Endurance/Patience

To bear difficult and painful experiences, situations or persons with calm, stability and perseverance.

Equality/Liberation

To experience yourself as having the same value and rights as all other human beings in such a way that you are set free to be yourself and to free others to be themselves.

Equilibrium

To maintain a peaceful social environment by averting upsets and avoiding conflicts.

Equity/Rights

To have an awareness of the moral and ethical claim of all persons (including yourself) to legal, social and economic equality and fairness plus a personal commitment to advocate this claim.

Evaluation/Self-System

To appreciate an objective appraisal of yourself. To be open to what others reflect back to you as being necessary for self-awareness and personal growth.

Expressiveness/Freedom/Joy

To share your feelings and fantasies so openly and spontaneously that others feel free to do the same.

Faith/Risk/Vision

To commit to a cause, or to champion a way of life, even if it may mean putting your lifestyle at risk.

Family/Belonging

To devote yourself to, or be concerned about, your family. To belong to and be accepted by your family. To have a place to call home.

Fantasy/Play

To experience your personal worth through unrestrained imagination and personal amusement.

Food/Warmth/Shelter

To have adequate physical nourishment, warmth and comfort and a place of refuge from the elements. To be protected from the natural elements.

Friendship/Belonging

To have friends to share things with on a day-to-day basis.

Function/Physical

To be able to perform minimal manipulations of your body to care for yourself. To be concerned about the body's internal systems and their ability to function adequately.

Generosity/Service

The desire to share your unique gifts and skills with others as a way of serving humanity without expecting anything in return.

Growth/Expansion

To creatively enable an organisation to develop and expand.

Health/Healing/Harmony

To have a soundness of mind and body that flows from meeting your emotional and physical needs through self-awareness and disciplined preventive measures.

Hierarchy/Propriety/Order

To have a methodical, harmonious arrangement of persons and things, ranked above one another, in conformity with established standards of what is good and proper within an organisation.

Honour

To have high respect for the worth, merit or rank of those in authority, e.g. parents, superiors or national leaders.

Human Dignity

The basic right of every human being to have respect and to have their basic needs met in a way that will allow them the opportunity to develop their potential.

Human Rights/World Order

To create the means for every person in the world to experience their basic right to life-giving resources such as food, shelter, employment, health and a minimal practical education.

Independence

To think and act for yourself in matters of opinion, conduct etc., without being subject to external constraint or authority.

Integration/Wholeness

To organise your personality (mind and body) into a coordinated, harmonious totality.

Interdependence

To value personal and inter-institutional cooperation above individual decision-making.

Intimacy

To be able to share yourself fully — thoughts, feelings, fantasies and realities — mutually and freely with another on a regular basis.

Intimacy/Solitude as Unitive

To experience the personal harmony that results from a combination of meditative practice, mutual openness and total acceptance of another. The experience leads to new levels of meaning and awareness of truth.

Justice/Global Distribution

To elicit inter-institutional and governmental collaboration to help provide the basic life necessities for the poor in the world.

Justice/Social Order

To see every human being as being of equal value and to place a priority on taking a course of action that addresses, confronts and helps correct conditions of human oppression.

Knowledge/Discovery/Insight

To be motivated by the experience of moments of insight in a quest for truth through patterned investigation.

Law/Guide

To see authoritative principles and regulations as a means for creating your own criteria and moral conscience, and questioning those rules until they are clear and meaningful to you.

Law/Rule

To live life by the rules. To govern your conduct, action and procedures by the established legal system.

Leisure/Freesence

To use your time in a way that requires as much skill and concentration as your work, yet totally detaches you from work so that your spontaneous self is free to emerge in a playful and contagious manner.

Life/Self-Actualisation

To experience and express the totality of your being through spiritual, psychological, physical and mental exercises with the goal of developing your full potential.

Limitation/Acceptance

To give positive acceptance to the fact that people have weaknesses and limitations. To see their limitations as a necessary consequence of their strengths.

Limitation/Celebration

To recognise that your limitations are part of the framework for exercising your talents. To have the ability to laugh at your own imperfections.

Loyalty/Fidelity

To see as important the strict observance of promises and duties to those in authority and to those in close personal relationships.

Macroeconomics/World Order

To manage and direct the use of financial resources at an institutional and inter-institutional level. The goal being the creation of a more stable and equitable world economic order.

Management

To control and direct personnel in a business or institution for the purpose of optimal productivity and efficiency.

Membership/Institution

To take pride in belonging to and functioning as an integral part of an organisation, foundation, establishment, etc.

Minessence

To miniaturise and simplify complex ideas or technology into concrete and practical applications for the purpose of creatively impacting on the world-view of the user.

Mission/Objectives

To establish organisational goals and execute long-term planning that takes into consideration the needs of society and how the organisation contributes to those needs.

Mutual Responsibility/Accountability

To maintain a reciprocal balance of tasks and assignments with others so that everyone is answerable for their own area of responsibility.

Obedience/Duty

Dutiful and submissive compliance with moral and legal obligations established by parents, civic or religious authorities.

Obedience/Mutual Accountability

To be mutually and equally responsible for establishing and complying with a common set of rules and guidelines in a group.

Ownership

Personal and legal possession of skills, decisions and property that gives you a sense of personal authority.

Patriotism/Esteem

To honour your country through personal devotion, love and support.

Personal Authority/Honesty

To be in the position of being able to honestly express your full range of feelings and thoughts in a straightforward, objective manner. To command authority in your area of expertise.

Physical Delight

To delight in the joy of experiencing the stimulation of all the senses of your body, e.g. having a massage, sunbathing, taking a spa bath.

Pioneerism/Innovation

To introduce and originate creative ideas for positive change in organisations and other social systems. To provide the framework for implementing them.

Play/Recreation

To engage in an undirected, spontaneous pastime or diversion from the anxiety of daily life. To 'recharge your batteries' through playful activities.

Presence/Dwelling

To be there for another person in such a way that, through your own self-knowledge and inner wisdom, they are able to perceive themselves with increased clarity.

Prestige/Image

To have a physical appearance which reflects your success and achievement, gains the esteem of others and promotes success.

Productivity

To feel energised by generating and completing tasks and activities. To be keen to achieve the goals set for you by others and to live up to their expectations.

Property/Control

To accumulate property, and exercise personal control over it, for your security and to meet your basic physical and emotional needs.

Prophet/Vision

To perceive with clarity global issues of social justice, human rights, ecology, etc. To communicate your vision in relation to these issues with such clarity that your listeners are empowered by it to take action.

Relaxation

A diversion from physical or mental work which reduces stress and provides a balance of work and play as a means of realising your potential.

Research/Originality/Knowledge

The systematic investigation and contemplation of the nature of truths and principles that lie behind our experience of reality. The aim is to create new insights and awareness — to see things as no one has before.

Responsibility

To be personally accountable for, and in charge of, a specific area or course of action in your group or organisation.

Rights/Respect

To respect the rights and property of others as you expect them to respect you and yours.

Ritual Communication

To use liturgy and the arts as a communication medium for raising people's critical awareness of social issues.

Rule/Accountability

To have each person openly explain or justify their behaviour in relation to established codes of conduct, procedures, standards, etc.

Safety/Survival

To avoid personal injury, danger, or loss, and to do what is necessary to protect yourself in adverse circumstances.

Search/Meaning/Hope

The inner longing and curiosity to integrate your feelings, imagination and knowledge in order to discover your unique place in the world. To search for 'your place in the scheme of things'.

Security

To have a safe place or relationship where you experience protection and freedom from cares and anxieties. A place you find comforting to have.

Self-Interest/Control

To restrain your feelings and control your personal interests for the purpose of physical survival in this world.

Self-Preservation

To do whatever is necessary to protect yourself from physical harm or destruction in what you perceive as an alien/threatening world. To look after 'number one' in the face of threat.

Self-Worth

The knowledge that when those you respect and esteem really know you, they will affirm you are worthy of their respect.

Sensory Pleasure/Sexuality

To gratify your sensual desires and fully express your sexuality.

Service/Vocation

To use your unique gifts, skills and abilities to contribute to society through your occupation, business, profession or calling.

Sharing/Listening/Trust

To actively and accurately hear and sense another's thoughts and feelings. To express your own thoughts and feelings in a climate of mutual trust and confidence in each other's integrity.

Simplicity/Play

To have a deep appreciation of the world combined with a playful attitude toward organisations and systems that people find energising and positive. To see simplicity in complexity and to be detached from the material world.

Social Affirmation

Personal respect and validation, arising from the support and respect of your peers, which is necessary for your growth and success.

Support/Peer

To be sustained, in both joyful and difficult times, by persons similar to yourself.

Synergy

The harmonious and energising relationship of persons in a group that results in the group far surpassing its predicted ability (based on the summation of the abilities of its individual members).

Technology/Science

Systematic knowledge of the physical or natural world and practical applications of the knowledge through the construction of devices and tools.

Territory/Security
To make provision for physically defending your property, state or nation.

Tradition
To ritualise family history, religious history or national history in your life so as to enrich its meaning. To pass on traditional ways through ritual and ceremony.

Transcendence/Global Equality
To transcend physical needs with the intention of influencing issues of equality. For example a hunger strike to change the conditions for the inmates in a prison.

Truth/Wisdom/Integrated Insight
The intense pursuit and discovery of ultimate truth above all other activities. To seek the wisdom that stems from understanding a set of universal principles that govern all things.

Unity/Diversity
To value groups, organisations, society and the ecosystem, that have a diversity of membership. To value biodiversity.

Unity/Uniformity
To create harmony and agreement in an institution to the end of achieving efficiency, order, loyalty and conformity to established norms.

Wonder/Awe/Fate
To be filled with marvel, amazement and awe when faced with the overwhelming grandeur and power of your physical environment. To feel that, at times, things are out of your hands and fate rules.

Wonder/Curiosity/Nature

To experience the physical world with marvel and wonder. To seek to learn about and explore it personally.

Word

The desire to communicate universal truths so effectively that the listeners become conscious of their strengths and limitations and life and hope are renewed for each individual.

Work/Labour

To have the skills and rights enabling you to produce an adequate living for yourself and your family.

Workmanship/Craft/Art

To create products or works of art to enhance the world and our life in it.

Worship/Faith/Creed

Reverence for and belief in God that is expressed and experienced through a commitment to religious doctrines and teachings.

Bibliography and Recommended Reading

Allport, G.W. (1961), *Pattern and Growth in Personality,* Holt Rinehart and Winston, New York.

Andrews, Cecile (1997), *The Circle of Simplicity: Return to the good life*, HarperCollinsPublishers, New York.

Barker, Joel Arthur (1992), *Future Edge: Discovering the new paradigm of success*, William Morrow, New York.

Bryan, Mark and Cameron, Julia (1999*), Money Drunk, Money Sober: 90 days to financial freedom*, Ballantine Books, New York.

Colins, Clare and Chippendale, Paul (1995), *New Wisdom II: Values-based development*, Acorn Publications, Brisbane.

Cooper, Robert and Sawaf, Ayman (1997), *Executive EQ: Emotional intelligence in business*, Orion, London.

Csikszentmihalyi, Mihaly (1992), *Flow: the psychology of happiness*, Rider, London.

Dilts, Robert (1996), *Visionary Leadership Skills: Creating a world to which people want to belong*, Meta Publications, California.

Domingues, Joe and Robin, Vicki (1999), *Your Money or Your Life*, Penguin, New York.

Douillard, John (1994), *Body, Mind and Sport: The mind body guide to lifelong fitness and your personal best*, Crown, New York.

Frankl, Viktor (2000), *Man's Search for Meaning*, Beacon Press, Boston.

Fritz, Robert (1989), *The Path of Least Resistance: Learning to become the creative force in your own life*, Fawcett Books, New York.

Fritz, Robert (1999), *The Path of Least Resistance for Managers: Designing organisations to succeed*, Berrett-Koehler, San Francisco.

Glasser, William (1984), *Control Theory: A new explanation of how we control our lives*, Harper & Row, New York.

Goldsmith, Walter and Clutterbuck, David (1998), *The Winning Streak Mark 2*, Orion, London.

Hawkins, David (1995), *Power vs Force: The hidden determinants of human behaviour*, Hay House, Sydney.

Henderson, M. (1996), *The Me Degree*, Minerva Press, London.

Hilliard, A.L. (1950), *The Forms of Value: The extension of a hedonistic axiology*, Columbia University Press, New York.

Holden, Robert (1994), *Living Wonderfully: A joyful guide to conscious creative living for today*, Thorsons, London.

Holdsworth, Leanne (2000), *A New Generation of Business Leaders,* Holdsworth Press, Christchurch.

Jaap, Tom (1986) *Enabling Leadership: Achieving results with people*, HRA Publications, London.

Kelly, Anthony and Sewell, Sandra (1988) *With Head Heart and Hands: Dimensions of community building*, Boolarong, Brisbane.

Kluckhohn, Clyde (1951), *Values and Value Orientation in the Theory of Action*, Cambridge Press, Cambridge.

Koch, Richard (1998), *The 80/20 Principle: The secret of achieving more with less*, Nicholas Brealey, London.

Konorski, Jerzy (1967), *Integrative Activity of the Brain*, Chicago Press, Chicago.

Miller, William C. (1999), *Flash of Brilliance: Inspiring creativity where you work*, Perseus, New York.

Najder, Z. (1975), *Values and Evaluation*, Oxford, New York.

O'Connor, Joseph and McDermott, Ian (2001), *Neuro Linguistic Programming*, Thorsons, London.

Palmer, Harry (1997), *Resurfacing: Techniques for exploring consciousness*, Star's Edge International, Florida.

Rokeach, Milton (1973), *The Nature of Human Values*, Free Press, New York.

Scott, Ted and Harker, Phil (1998), *Humanity at Work*, Phil Harker & Associates, Queensland.

Secretan, Lance H.K. (1997), *Reclaiming Higher Ground: Creating organisations that inspire the soul*, McGraw-Hill, New York.

Secretan, Lance H.K. (1998), *The Way of the Tiger: Gentle wisdom for turbulent times*, Thaler Corporation, Ontario.

Thompson, Kevin (1998), *Emotional Capital: Capturing hearts and minds to create lasting business success*, Capstone, Oxford.

Webster, Alan (2001), *Spiral of Values: The flow from survival to global consciousness in New Zealand*, Alpha Publications, Auckland.

Wright, Kurt (1998), *Breaking the Rules: Removing the obstacles to effortless high performance*, CPM Publishing, Boise.

Wrycza, Peter (1997), *Living Awareness: Awakening the roots of learning and perception*, Gateway Books, Bath.

Values at Work

How many companies create a fancy vision statement, hang it on the wall and never refer to it again? For all the hype, identifying company values is worthwhile only if management then refer to these values in all business decisions, and motivate employees to do the same.

Values at Work takes the theories underpinning the authors' successful consulting practice and sets them out for the business manager seeking to:

- identify company values;
- coach staff to implement those values in the day-to-day running of the business;
- support staff in identifying their own personal values and comparing them to those of the company.

Including interviews with company executives already implementing values-based management techniques, *Values at Work* provides a practical guide for managers seeking to understand values and their impact on people, performance and profit.

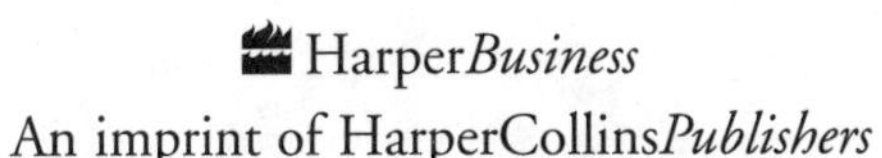

values@work

If you have enjoyed in this book and are interested in obtaining more information about values processes in order to develop yourself or your organisation, then please contact the team at values @ work on +64 9 372 2045 or email truenorth@valuesatwork.org